French - Korean

LEARNING FLASHCARDS

FOR BABIES TODDLERS

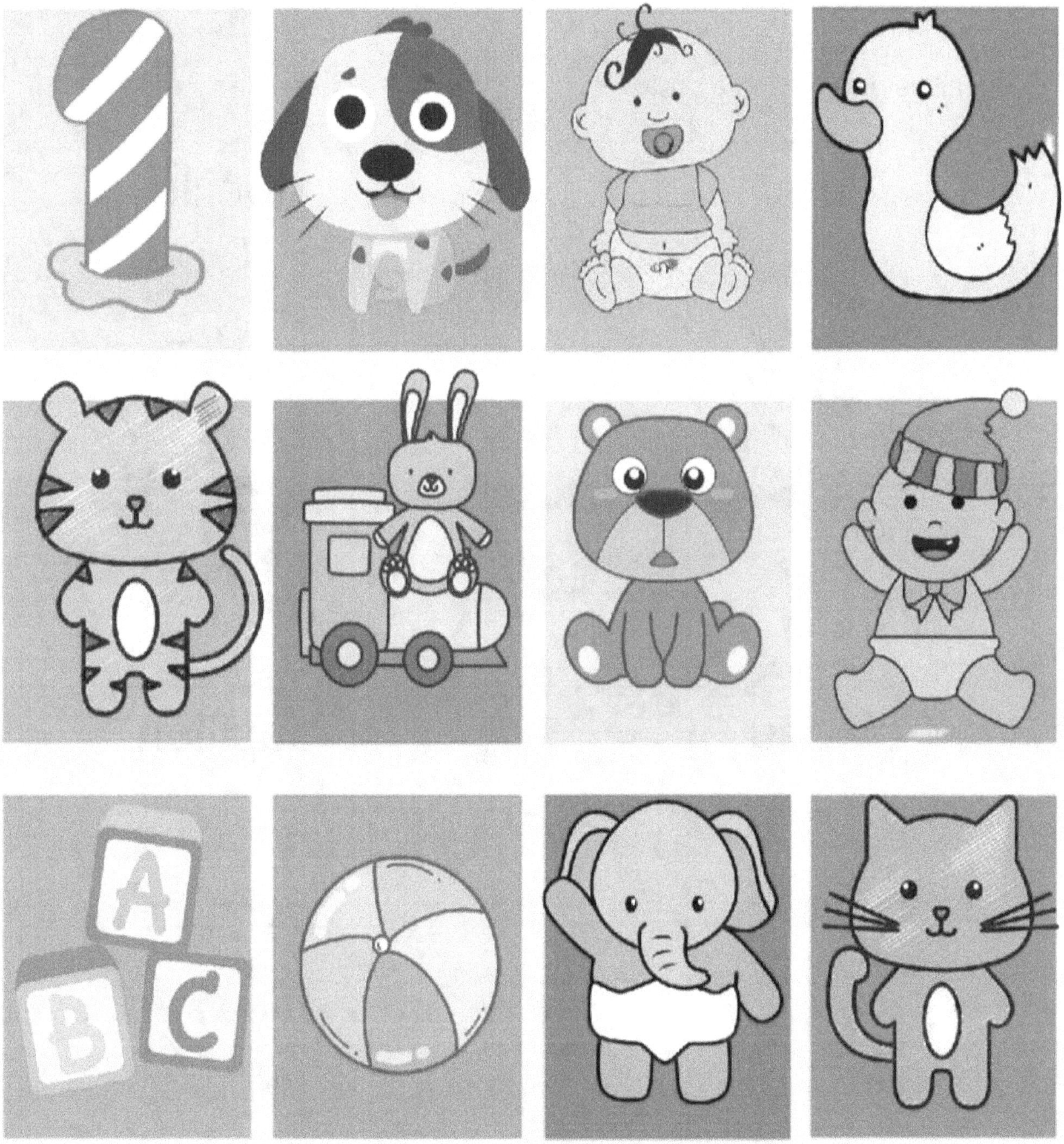

alligator

악어

The alligator is having a party.

fourmi

개미

The ant is red.

ours

곰

The bear loves you.

abeille

벌

The bee is saying hello.

oiseau

새

The bird is flying.

papillon

나비

The butterfly is pretty.

chameau

낙타

The camel has a hump.

chat

고양이

The cat is happy.

dinosaure

공룡

The dinosaur is laying eggs.

poulet

치킨

The chicken is dancing.

vache

소

The cow has a bell.

cerf

사슴

The reindeer has a toy.

chien

개

The dog has two floppy ears.

dauphin

돌고래

The dolphin is swimming.

canard

오리

The duck has a bow.

aigle

독수리

The eagle is looking for food.

l'éléphant

코끼리

The elephant is sitting.

poisson

물고기

The fish is a clownfish.

libellule

잠자리

The dragonfly is blue.

renard

여우

The fox has a red nose.

grenouille

개구리

The frog is smiling.

girafe

기린

The giraffe has a long neck.

chèvre

염소

The goat has a beard

ver de terre

벌레

The worm is in the apple

poule

암탉

The hen has chicks.

hippopotame

하마

The hippo is big.

cheval

말

The horse is fast.

kangourou

캥거루

The kangaroo has a baby.

chaton

고양이 새끼

The kitten is playing.

lion

사자

The lion has a mane.

homard

랍스터

The lobster is red.

singe

원숭이

The monkey has a tail.

poulpe

문어

The octopus has food.

hibou

올빼미

The owls have big eyes.

panda

팬더

The panda wears a diaper.

porc

돼지

The pig is fat and pink.

chiot

강아지

The dog is brown.

lapin

토끼

The rabbit has a carrot.

rat

쥐

The mouse is writing something.

crabe

게

The crab has two pinchers.

requin

상어

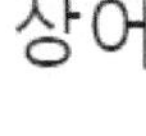

The shark is scary.

mouton

양

The sheep are very fluffy.

escargot

달팽이

The snail is slow.

serpent

뱀

The snake has poison.

araignée

거미

The spider is purple.

écureuil

청설모

The squirrel has a nut.

tigre

호랑이

The tiger has a red bow.

tortue

터틀

The turtle has a shell.

loup

늑대

The wolf is smiling.

zèbre

얼룩말

The zebra is black and white.

dinde

터키

The turkey has two legs.

coq

수탉

The rooster will crow.

perroquet

앵무새

The parrot is colorful.

hérisson

고슴도치

The hedgehog has apples.

pomme

사과

The apple has a leaf.

abricot

살구

The apricot is yellow.

avocat

아보카도

The avocado has a nut.

banane

바나나

The banana is yellow.

la mûre

블랙 베리

There are a lot of blackberries.

cassis

까치밥 나무

The blackcurrants are yummy.

myrtille

블루 베리

The blueberries are sweet.

cerise

체리

The cherries have a stem.

noix de coco

코코넛

The coconuts have juice.

figues

무화과

The fig has seeds.

grain de raisin

포도

The grapes are purple.

pamplemousse

그레이프 프루트

The grapefruits are sour.

kiwi

키위

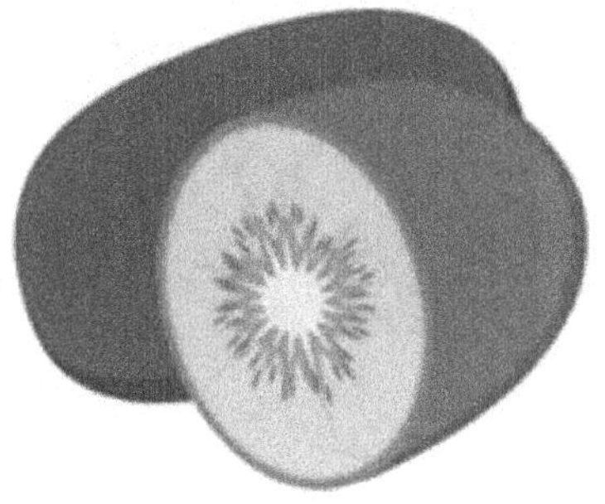

The kiwi is fresh.

citron

레몬

The lemons are yellow.

citron vert

라임

We have lots of lime.

litchi

그 열매

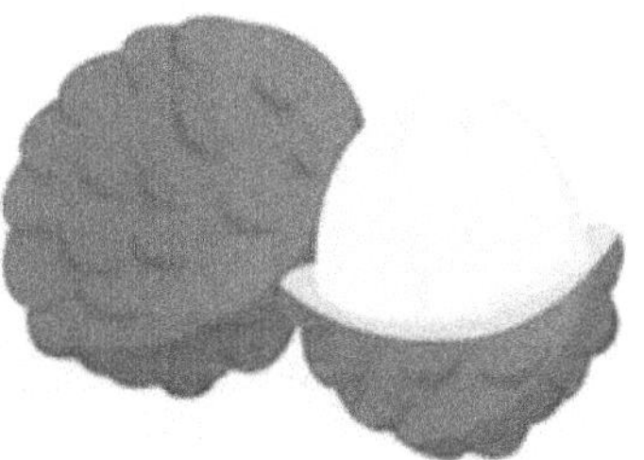

I like to eat lychee.

mandarine

만다린 오렌지

Oranges are refreshing.

mangue

망고

Mango is my favorite fruit.

orange

주황색

Mandarins are like oranges.

papaye

파파야

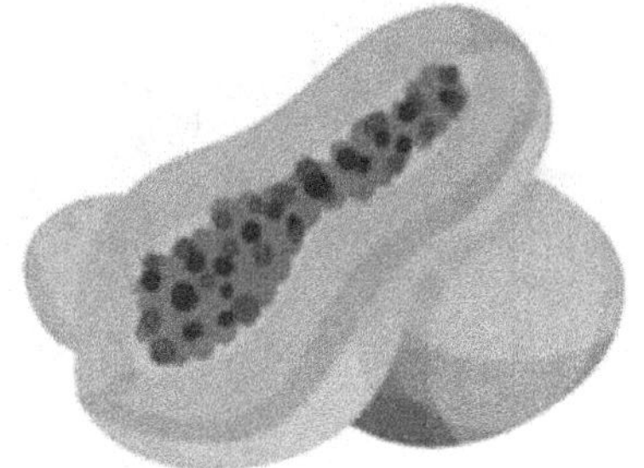

Papayas have lots of seeds.

pêche

복숭아

Peaches are juicy.

poire

배

Pears have a strange figure.

ananas

파인애플

The pineapple has a thumbs up.

prune

자두

Plums are healthy for you.

grenade

석류

Pomegranates are all red.

framboise

산딸기

The raspberry is shiny.

fraise

딸기

The strawberry has leaves on top.

pastèque

수박

The watermelon is big.

mandarine

귤

The tangerine looks like an orange.

tarte

파이

I like to eat apple pie.

gâteau

케이크

That cake is huge.

bonbons

사탕

Candy is not good for your teeth.

biscuit

쿠키

Cookies are easy to make.

donut

도넛

I like strawberry donuts.

crème glacée

아이스크림

The ice cream is melting.

muffin

머핀

The muffin has a cute wrapper.

pudding

푸딩

We eat pudding on Christmas.

classeur

접합재

I keep pictures in my binder.

livre

책

I like to eat books.

sac à dos

배낭

The backpack has lots of stuff.

les ciseaux

가위

I have scissors in my bag.

épingles

다리

Pins can hold stuff up.

agrafe

클립

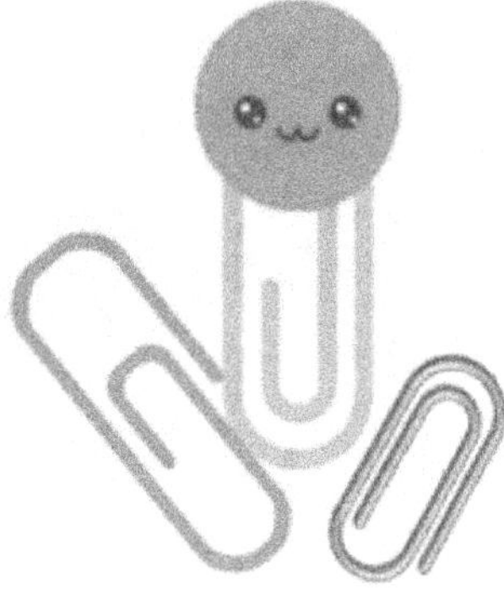

Clips can hold up paper.

papier

종이

I have lots of paper.

agrafeuse

호치키스

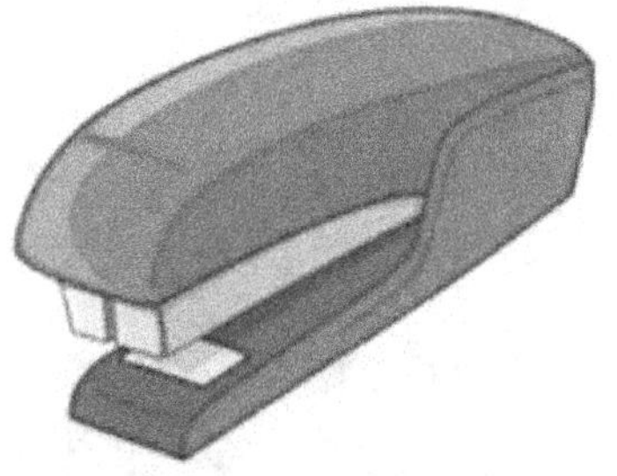

My stapler is shiny and red.

calculatrice

계산자

My calculator has buttons.

règle

지배자

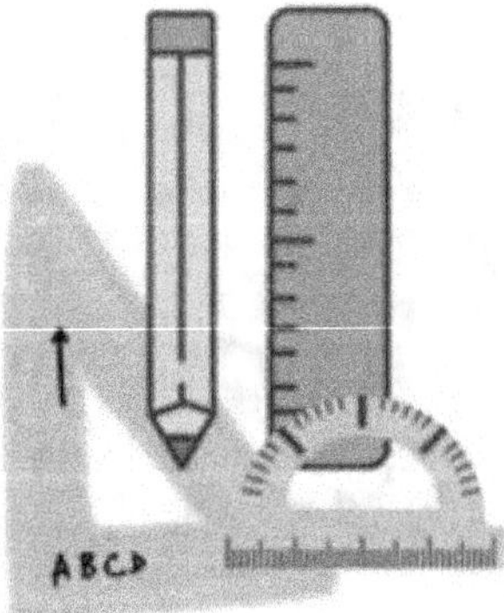

I have lots of rulers.

la colle

접착제

The glue is sticky.

bibliothèque

책장

My bookcase has lots of things.

calendrier

달력

I have a calendar on my table.

chaise

의자

My chair is fancy.

l'horloge

시계

The clock says that it's 3 o'clock.

ordinateur

컴퓨터

I do things on my computer.

bureaux

책상

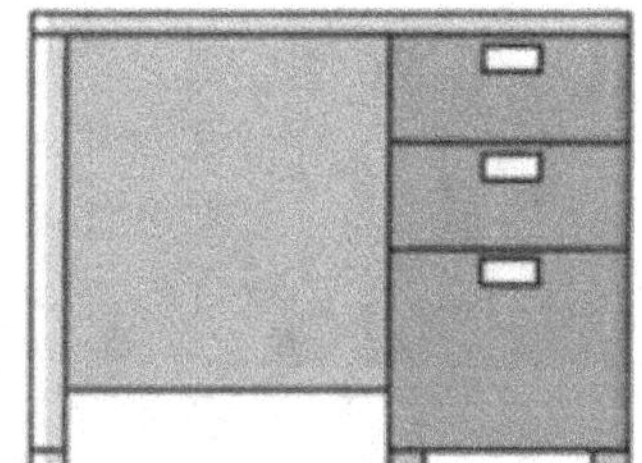

I put lots of things on my desk.

dictionnaire

사전

The dictionary has lots of words.

la gomme

지우개

Erasers are used with pencils.

carte

지도

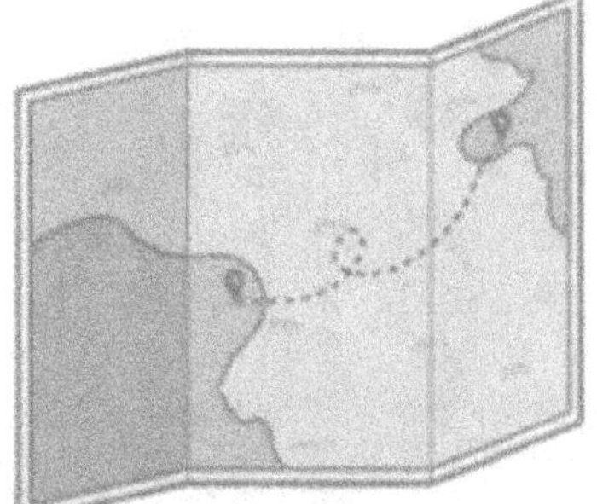

The map shows you different places.

carnet

공책

I use notebooks at school.

stylo

펜

My pen is very pretty.

crayon

연필

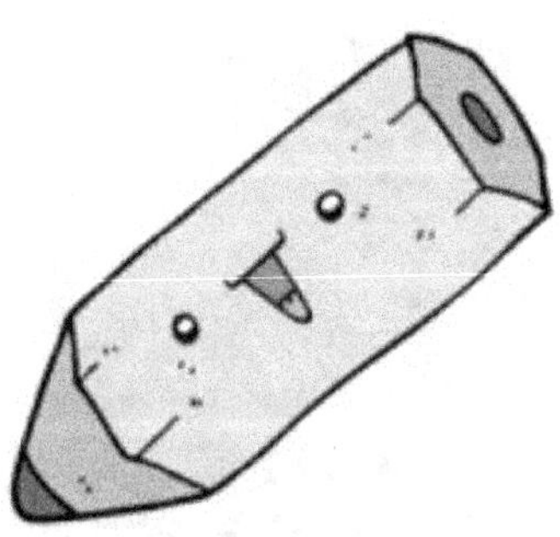

My friend gave me a pencil.

ceinture

벨트

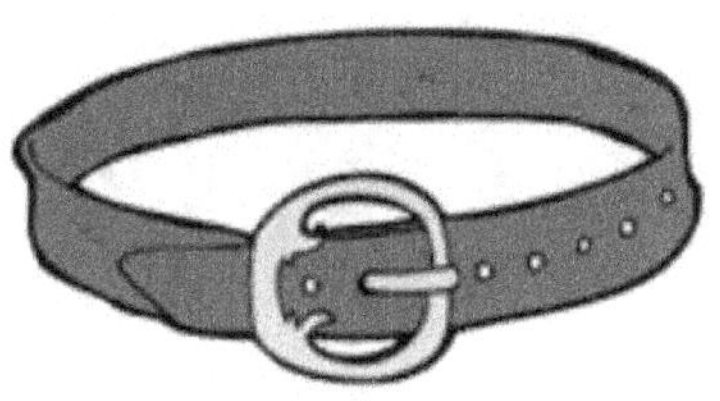

I have a belt on my pants.

bottes

부츠

I have big brown boots.

chapeau

모자

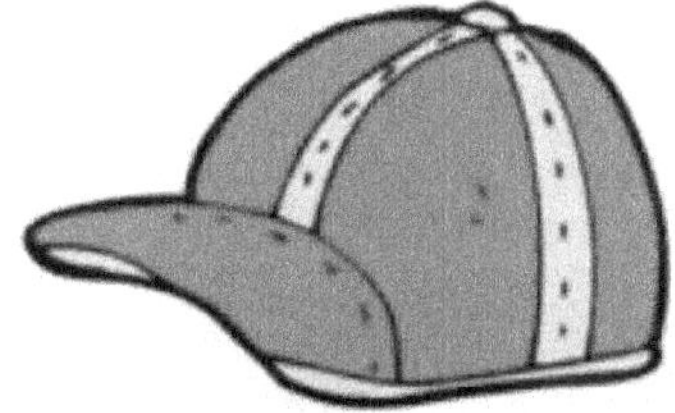

My mom bought me a new cap.

manteau

코트

She has a long yellow coat.

robes

복장

My dress has a bow.

gants

장갑

I got new gloves.

chapeau

모자

That hat is for a wicked witch.

veste

재킷

The jacket is cozy.

jeans

청바지

My jeans are long.

pyjamas

잠옷

I sleep in my pajamas.

un pantalon

바지

The bear is wearing pants.

imperméable

비옷

We wear our raincoats when it is raining.

écharpe

스카프

The baby has a scarf around his neck.

chemise

셔츠

I like this shirt the best.

des chaussures

신발

I have red and blue shoes.

jupe

치마

My skirt has lots of buttons.

pantalon

느슨한 바지

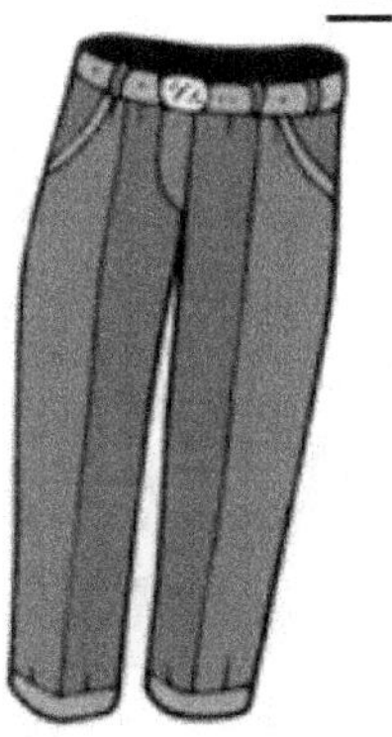

My dad wears slacks.

chaussons

슬리퍼

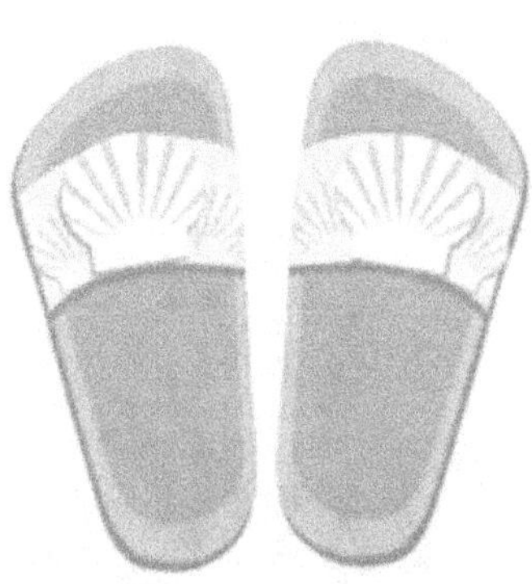

I have seashells on my sandals.

chaussettes

양말

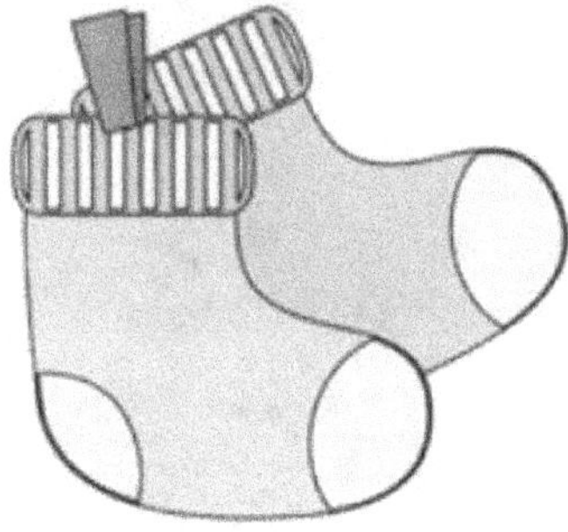

My baby sister wears socks.

costume

소송

My brother is wearing a suit.

chandail

스웨터

I am wearing a sweater for winter.

cravate

넥타이

My dad wears a tie to meetings.

pantalon

바지

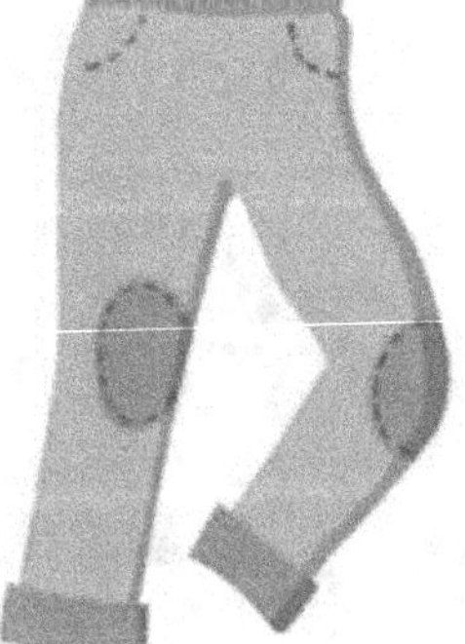

The trousers look like jeans.

slip

팬티

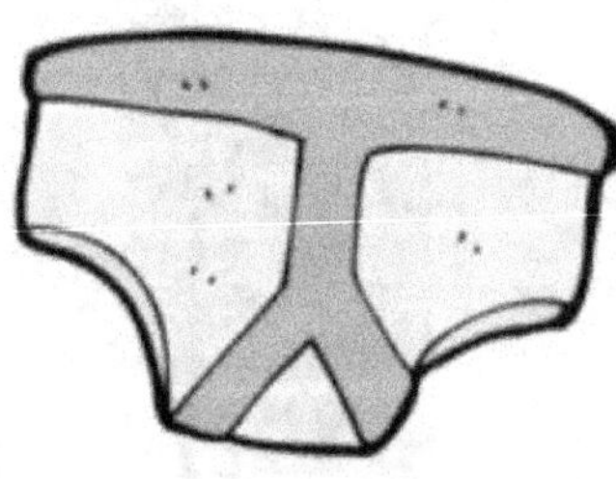

I always wear my underwear.

maillot de corps

땀받이

My undershirt has a star.

une

하나

Number one and the bee are friends.

deux

두

The cat and the mouse both love two.

trois

세

The bear gives number three a present.

quatre

네

Number four is a home for the cat.

cinq

다섯

Number five hatches an egg.

six

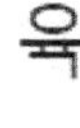

육

Number six is going to eat a carrot.

sept

일곱

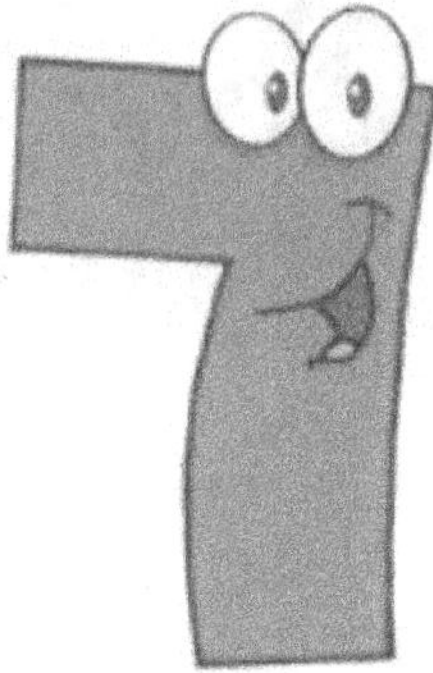

Number seven is playing with the tiger.

huit

여덟

Number eight is funny.

neuf

아홉

Number nine meets the parrot.

dix

십

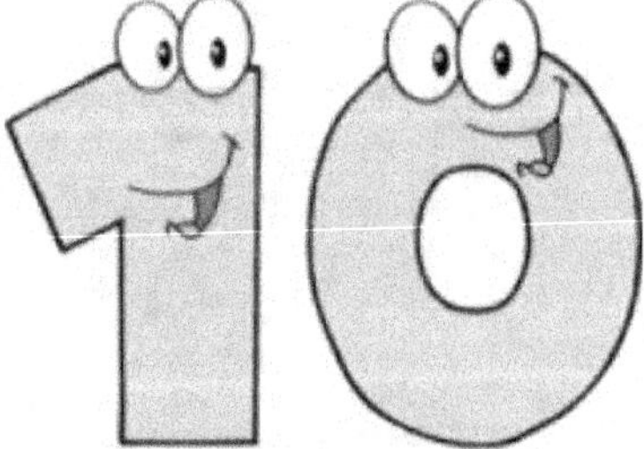

Number ten is smiling.

onze

열한

Number eleven has big eyes.

douze

열 두번째

Number twelve is number one and two.

treize

열셋

Number thirteen is excited.

quatorze

십사

The number fourteen is vast.

quinze

열 다섯

The number fifteen is green.

seize

열 여섯

Sixteen is my lucky number.

dix-sept

십칠

Number seventeen look alike.

dix-huit

십팔

Number eighteen will go to the circus.

dix-neuf

십구

I am nineteen now!

vingt

이십

Number twenty has a zero.

fourmi

개미

The ant has lots of legs.

cloche

벨

The bell will ring.

vache

소

The cow has a bow.

poupée

인형

She has a cute bear doll.

oeuf

계란

The chick has hatched out of the egg.

poisson

물고기

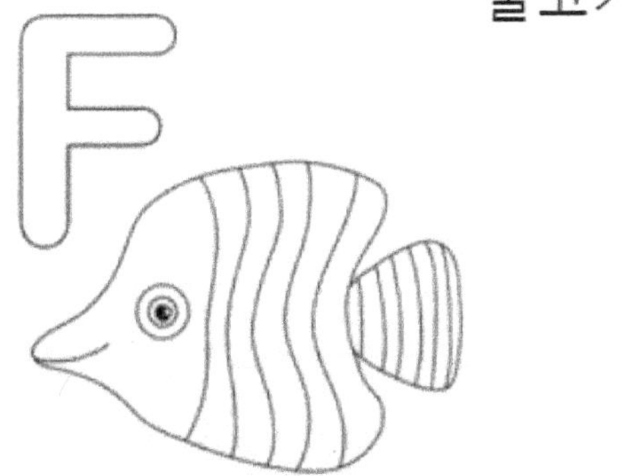

The fish is swimming in the water.

chèvre

염소

The goat is sitting on the grass.

chapeau

모자

He is wearing a hat.

crème glacée

아이스크림

I like to eat ice cream.

confiture

잼

The kitten is sitting on the jam jar.

chaton

고양이 새끼

The cat is sleeping on the floor.

lion

사자

The lion is waiting for the tiger.

rat

쥐

The mouse has lots of presents.

nez

코

The reindeer has a red nose.

hibou

올빼미

The owl is sleeping.

The pig will eat cupcakes.

The queen has a big crown.

The rabbit is jumping up and down.

The sheep have fluffy wool.

The turtle has a shell.

The mouse is holding an umbrella.

van

봉고차

The van is driving along the road.

pastèque

수박

The watermelon has lots of seeds.

xylophone

목금

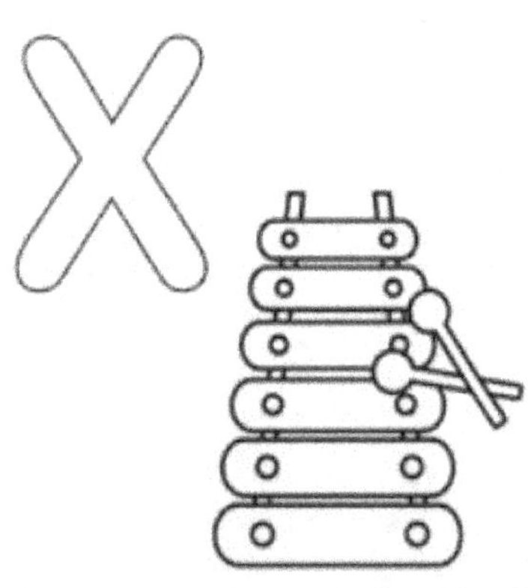

We are going to play the xylophone.

yaourt

요거트

We opened the yogurt can.

zèbre

얼룩말

The zebra is surprised.

rose

분홍

color the word and
the picture in pink

Most of my clothes are pink.

marron

갈색

color the word and
the picture in pink

brown

My chocolate is brown.

gris

회색

color the word and
the picture in pink

gray

I don't like the color gray.

vert

초록

color the word and
the picture in pink

green

The vegetables are green.

jaune

노랑

color the word and
the picture in pink

yellow

Bananas are yellow.

blanc

하얀

color the word and
the picture in pink

white

The paper that I write on is white.

rouge

빨간

color the word and
the picture in pink

red

Apples are red.

bleu

color the word and
the picture in pink

blue

The night sky is blue.

percer

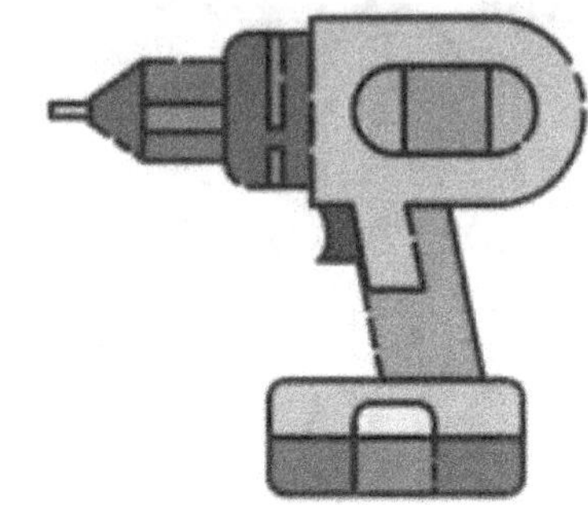

송곳

The drill will help us fix this.

marteau

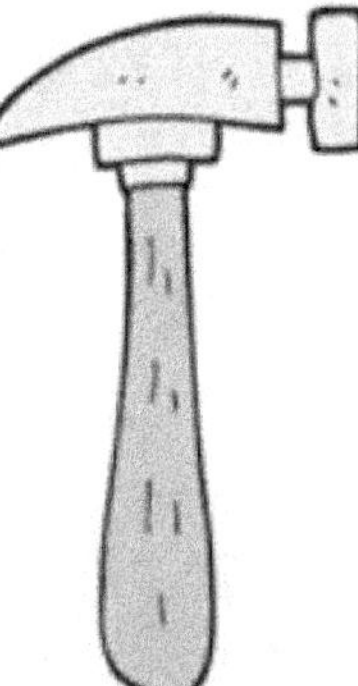

망치

The hammer is going to nail the picture.

couteau

칼

The knife is sharp.

pinces

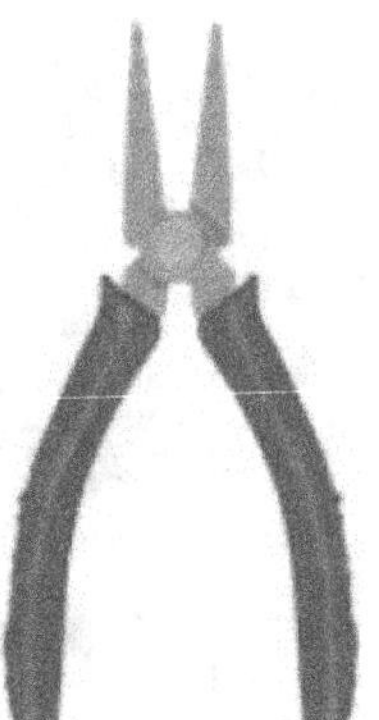

펜치

The plier is used for many things.

vu

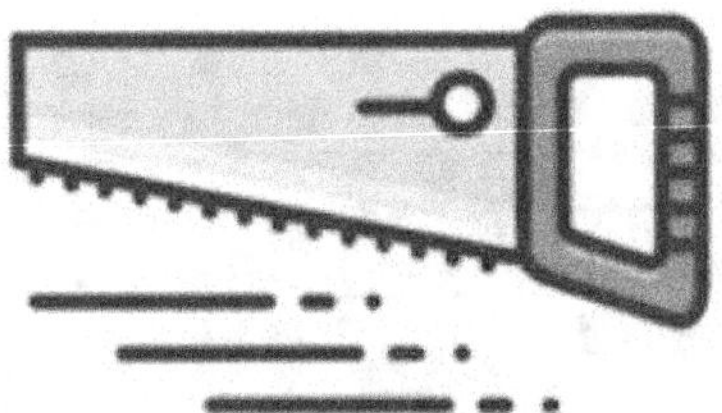

보았다

The saw can chop wood.

les ciseaux

가위

I use scissors to cut paper.

tournevis

드라이버

The screwdriver can screw in the knots.

clé

렌치

The wrench can help unscrew the knots.

avion

비행기

The airplane is going to leave now.

vélo

자전거

The bicycle is beautiful.

bateau

보트

The boat is floating on the water.

autobus

버스

The bus is going to school.

voiture

차

The car is green.

hélicoptère

헬리콥터

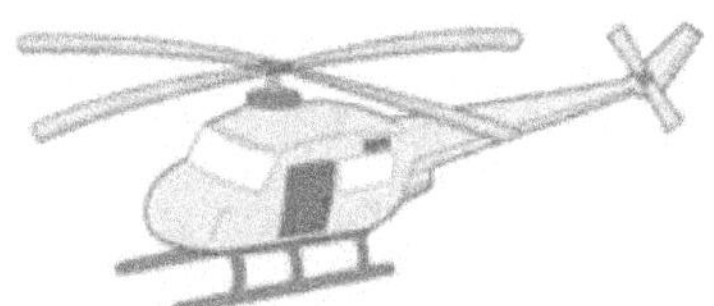

The helicopter is looking for
something.

cheval

말

You can ride the horse.

jet

제트기

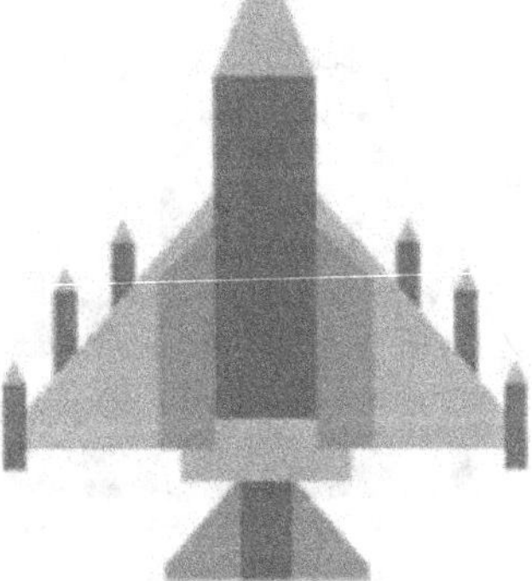

The jet is high-speed.

moto

오토바이

The motorcycle is on the road.

navire

배

The ship is on the water.

métro

지하철

My mom goes on the subway to work.

taxi

택시

The taxi has someone inside.

train

기차

The train is going slowly.

un camion

트럭

The truck has stuff in it.

asperges

아스파라거스

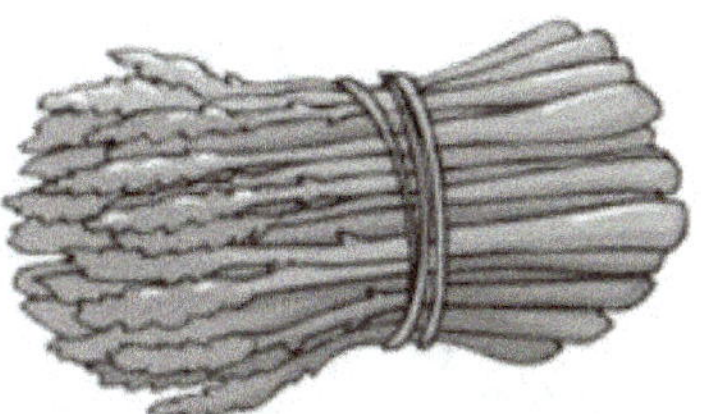

The asparagus is in a bundle.

des haricots

콩

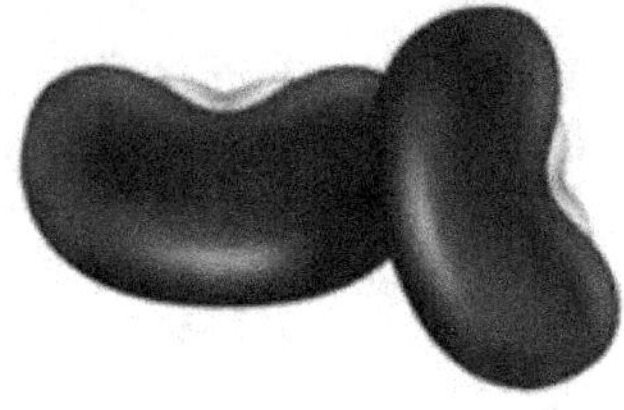

The beans are smooth.

brocoli

브로콜리

The broccoli is dancing.

chou

양배추

Bunnies like to eat cabbage.

carotte

당근

The carrots are very long.

céleri

셀러리

The celery has lots of leaves.

blé

옥수수

Corn soup is delicious.

concombre

오이

The cucumbers are cut into pieces.

aubergine

가지

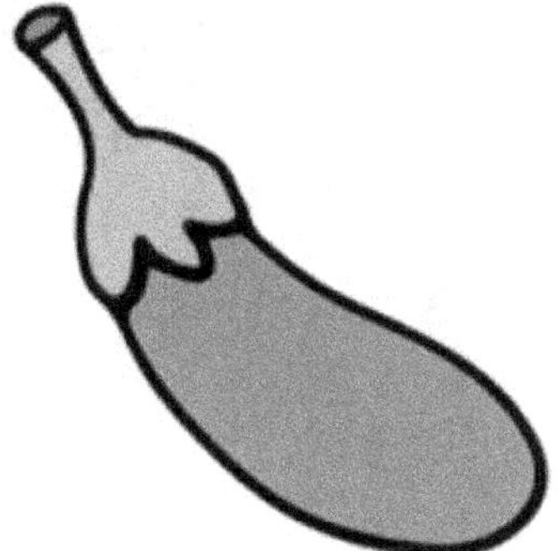

The eggplant is purple.

poivre vert

피망

The green pepper is juicy.

salade

상추

The lettuce is all green.

oignon

양파

The onions make my eyes water.

pois

완두콩

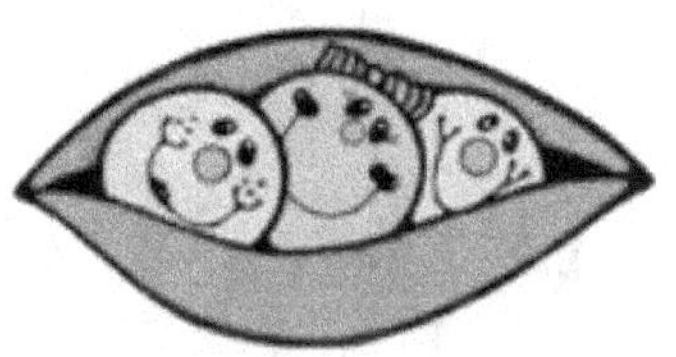

The peas are all in a pod.

patate

감자

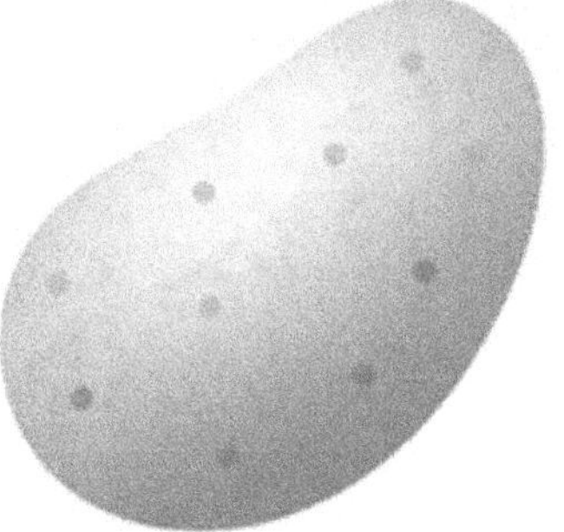

The potato is very shiny.

citrouille

호박

The pumpkin is for Halloween.

un radis

무

The radish is a type of vegetable.

épinard

시금치

The spinach is good with cheese.

patate douce

고구마

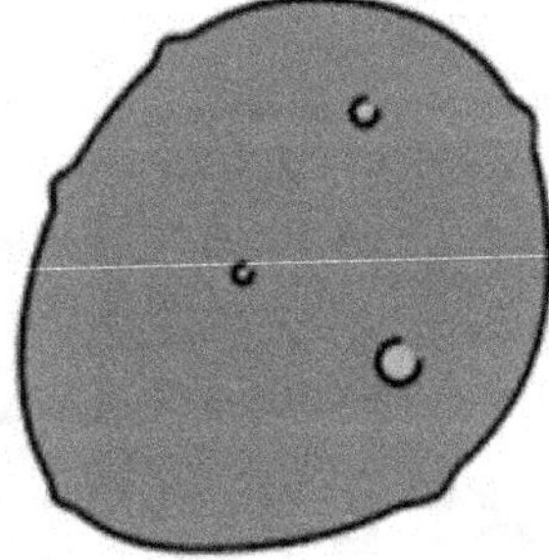

The sweet potato is quite sweet.

tomate

토마토

I don't like to eat tomatoes.

navet

순무

My mom bought some turnips.

nuageux

흐림

The weather is cloudy today.

du froid

춥다

I like cold weather.

cool

멋있는

The temperature is cold today.

brumeux

흐린

The fog is so strong I can't see the city.

chaud

뜨거운

The fire is burning hot.

humide

습한

It's so humid and wet today.

pluvieux

비오는

It's raining very hard.

neigeux

설원

Welcome to snow land!

orageux

폭풍우 같은

I hate the stormy weather.

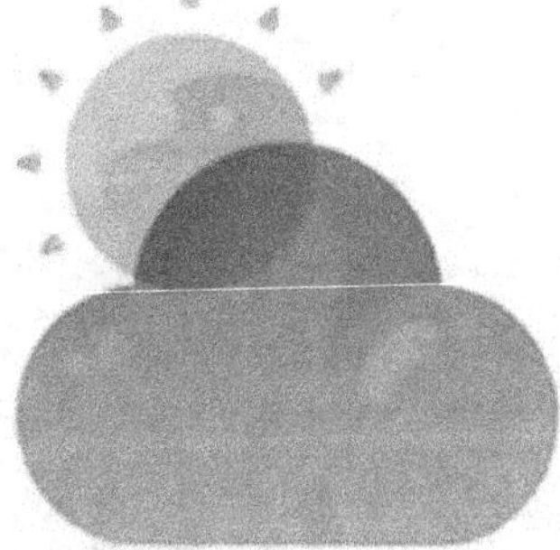

ensoleillé

햇볕이 잘 드는

The sun is shining!

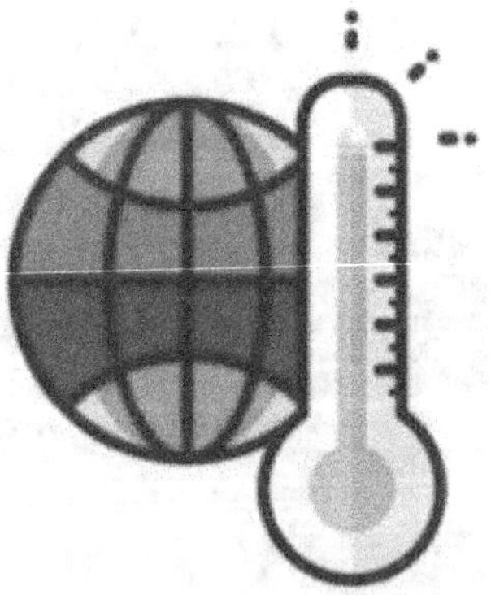

chaud

따뜻한

The whole world is warm today!

venteux

깜짝 놀란

The leaves are blowing away since it's so windy!

tante

이모

My aunt is very nice to me.

frère

동료

My brother is very fun to play with.

cousin

사촌

I love going to the playground with my cousin.

fille

딸

I like to read books with my daughter.

père

아버지

My father is playing with me.

petite fille

손녀

My granddaughter has blond hair.

grand-mère

할머니

My grandmother is very old and has glasses.

petit fils

손자

My grandson and I are very excited today!

mère

어머니

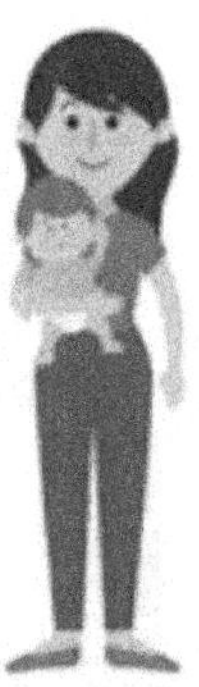

My mother likes to pick me up.

neveu

조카

My father's nephew is my cousin.

nièce

조카딸

My niece is very good at playing ball.

sœur

여자 형제

My sister is so pretty!

fils

아들

My son likes to play with toy cars.

belle fille

의붓 딸

My stepdaughter likes the color orange.

belle-mère

계모

My stepmother is pretty.

beau-fils

의붓 아들

This is my stepson, Greg.

oncle

삼촌

My uncle tells lots of funny jokes.

bol

사발

The bowl has nothing inside.

tasse

컵

My mom drinks her coffee out of a cup.

plat

요리

That dish has a bone inside.

fourchette

포크

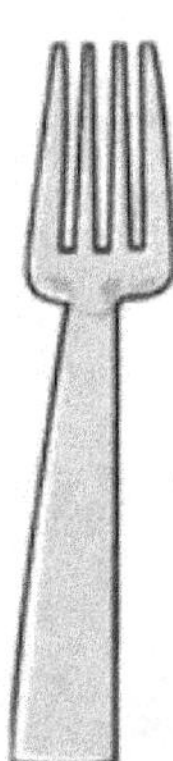

We have more spoons than forks.

verre

유리

I have a glass of water on my desk.

couteau

칼

I have a knife in my kitchen.

agresser

얼굴

This mug of coffee is for my dad.

serviette de table

냅킨

You can use the napkins to clean your hands.

poivre

후추

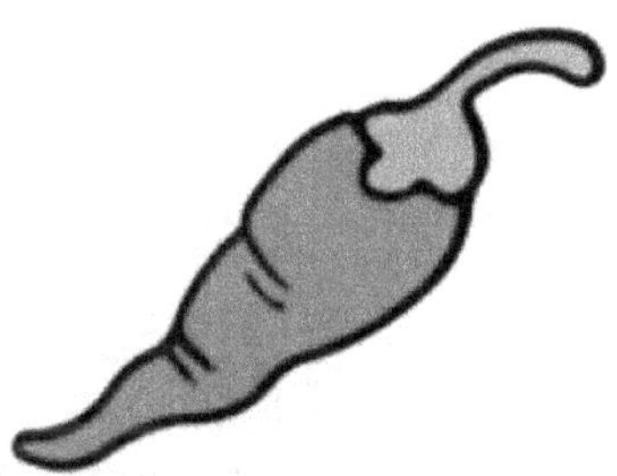

The pepper is very spicy.

lanceur

피처

Pour yourself some lemonade from the pitcher.

assiette

플레이트

Can you help me wash the plates?

salade

샐러드

The salad is very healthy for you.

sel

소금

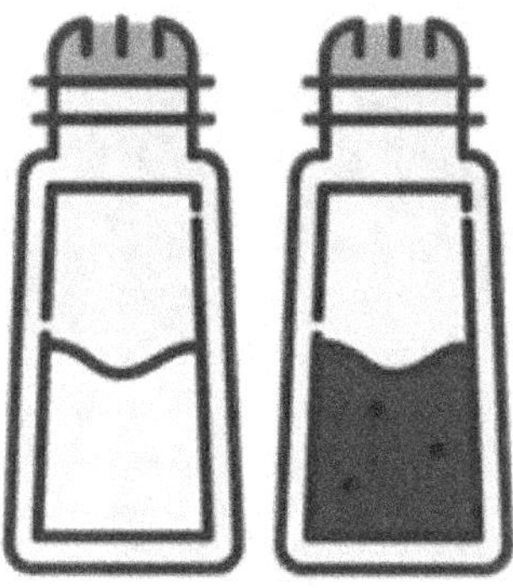

The salt tastes good with a few pinches of pepper.

soucoupe

받침 접시

The plate is for my cup.

cuillère

숟가락

I use a spoon to eat my rice.

sucre

설탕

The pack of sugar is very heavy.

dimanche

일요일

Sunday

Sunday is the day to go to Church!

lundi

월요일

Monday

Monday is the day to start school.

mardi

화요일

Tuesday

We will go to the shops on Tuesday.

mercredi

수요일

Wednesday

Wednesday is hard to spell!

jeudi

목요일

Thursday

Thursday is the fourth day of the week!

vendredi

금요일

Friday

My birthday is on Friday!

samedi

토요일

Saturday

Saturday is the weekend!

cuire

빵 굽기

The chef will bake a cake.

ébullition

종기

I will boil the eggs.

griller

굽다

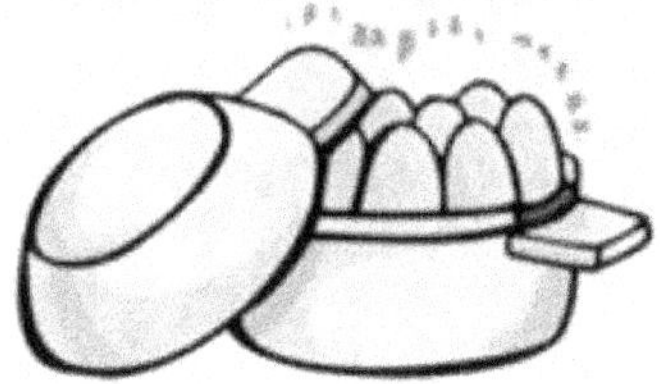

Broil is very yummy.

ouvre-boîte

병따개

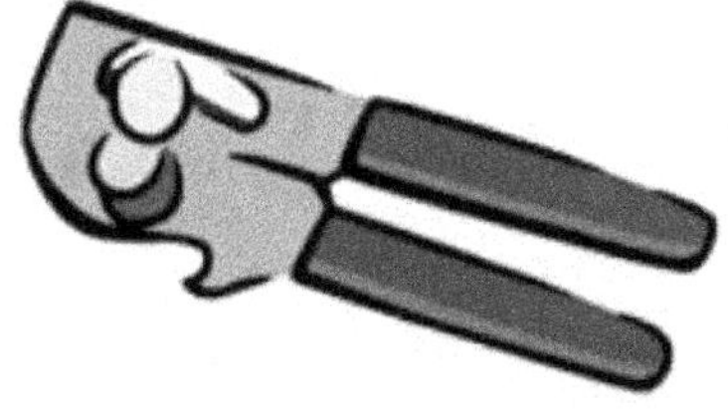

That can opener is used for opening cans.

frire

튀김

The pan can fry lots of things.

gril

그릴

We have a grill in our backyard.

tasse à mesurer

계량컵

My mom uses the measuring cup for baking.

cuillère à mesurer

계량 스푼

I use a measuring spoon to eat my dessert.

four micro onde

마이크로파

The microwave is used to heat food.

bol à mélanger

믹싱 보울

She is using the mixing bowl to mix things.

serviettes en papier

종이 타월

Dry your hands with paper towels.

poché aux œufs

계란 밀렵

The poach is put on noodles.

porte pot

냄비 손잡이

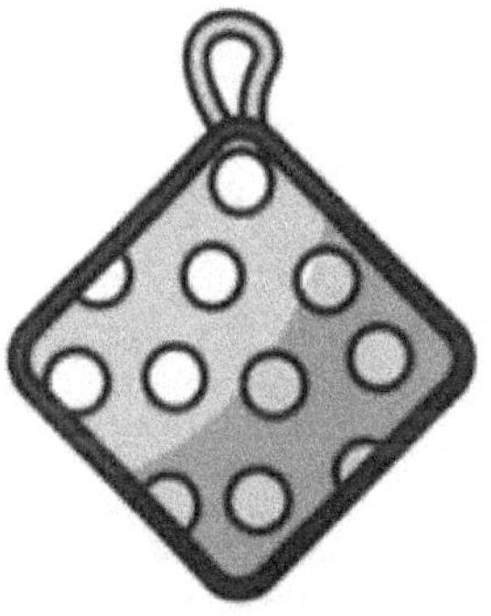

The potholder is soft.

rôti

구운

The chef made roast chicken.

rouleau à pâtisserie

롤링 핀

He is holding a rolling pin.

brouiller

스크램블

My mom is making scrambled eggs for breakfast.

mijoter

끓이다

The simmer is rice today.

couteau

칼

The knife is sharp.

cuillère

숟가락

I eat my food with a spoon and fork.

spatule

주걱

The spatula will help us flip the steak over.

vapeur

증기

The steam is coming from the pot.

passoire

거르는 사람

The strainer is used to strain stuff.

minuteur

시간제 노동자

I set my timer for 12:00.

fourchette

포크

I have lots of metallic forks.

grille-pain

토스터에

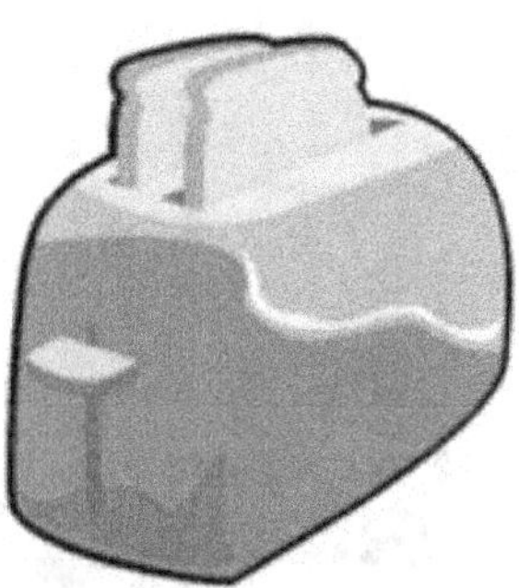

The toaster will toast my bread.

bouilloire

주전자

The kettle has tea inside.

réfrigérateur

냉장고

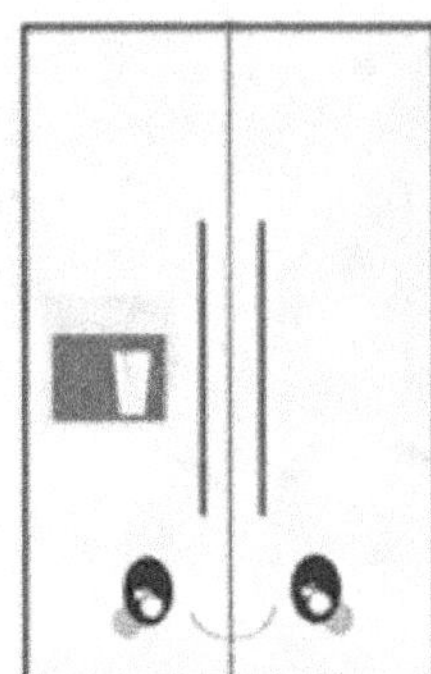

The refrigerator has lots of things inside.

mixeur

블렌더

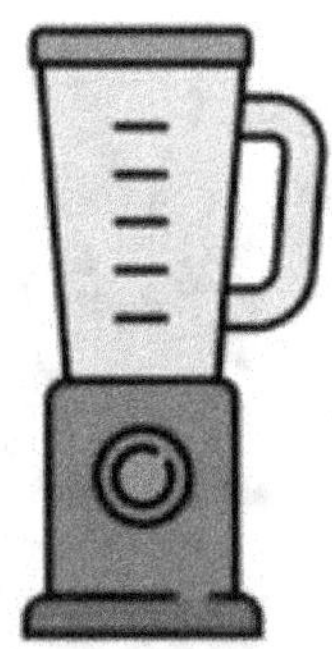

The blender will mix up my fruits.

cabinets

캐비닛

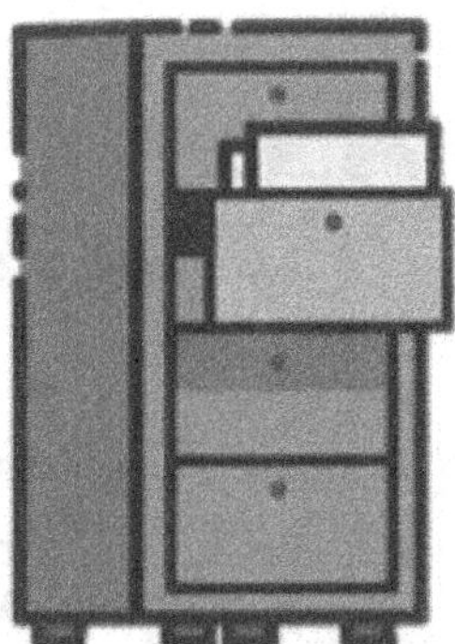

The cabinet has my paper inside.

placard

찬장

The cupboard has lots of books.

four micro onde

마이크로파

The microwave will heat my food.

arrière

뒤

She has a slender back.

des joues

궁둥이

She kisses her mom on the cheek.

poitrine

가슴

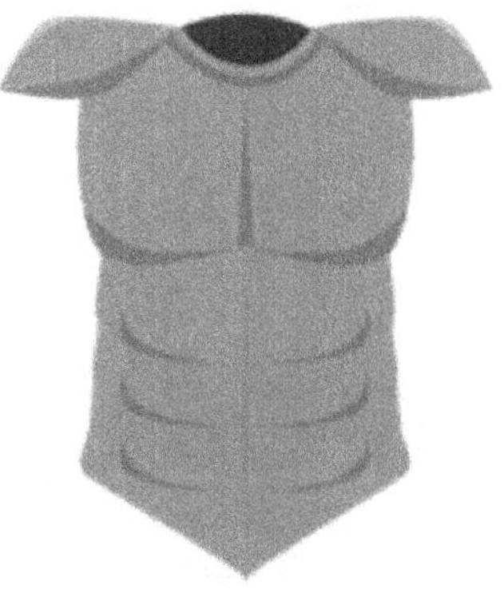

The armor is for your chest.

menton

턱

This is my chin!

oreilles

귀

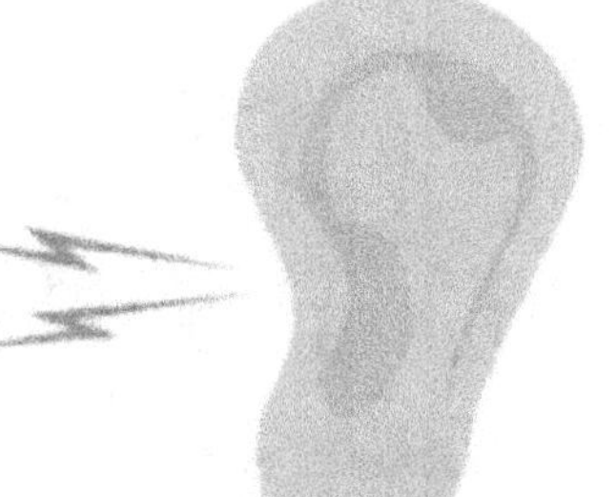

The ear is hearing something.

les sourcils

눈썹

The eyebrows are raised.

yeux

눈

The eyes are blue.

pieds

피트

I have one pair of feet.

des doigts

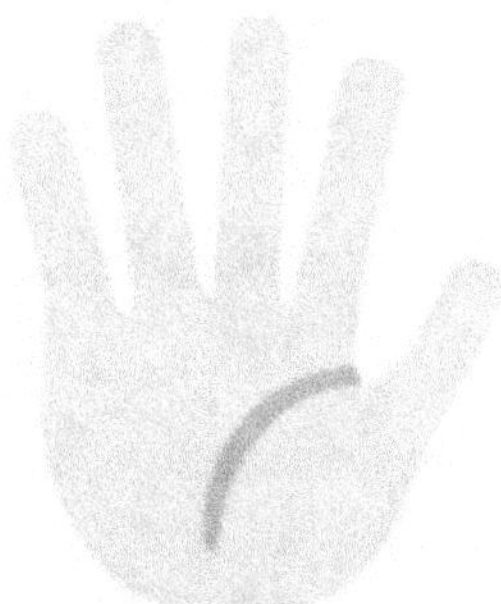

손가락

The fingers are waving at us.

pied

발

My foot has five fingers.

front

이마

My brain is behind my forehead.

cheveux

머리

My hair is long and black.

mains

소유

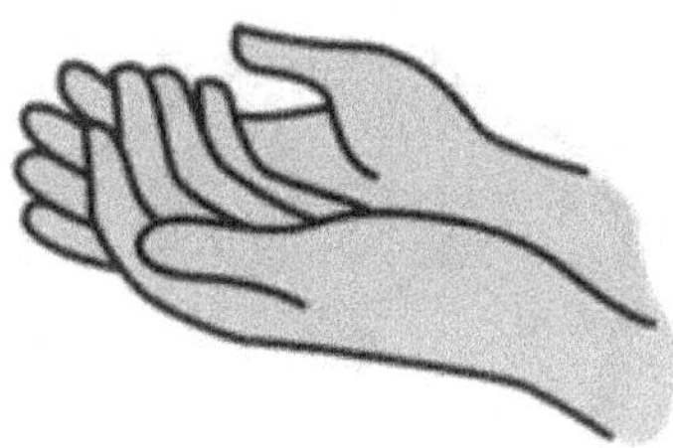

I will wash my hands in the sink.

tête

머리

She has a big head.

les hanches

엉덩이

The gorilla has his hands on his hips.

les genoux

무릎

She is begging on her knees.

jambes

다리

The tiger has strong legs.

lèvres

입술

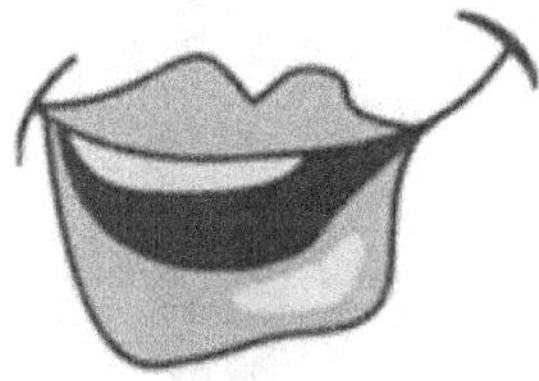

The lips have lipstick on.

bouche

입

He is covering his mouth with his hand.

cou

목

The necklace is very special to me.

nez

코

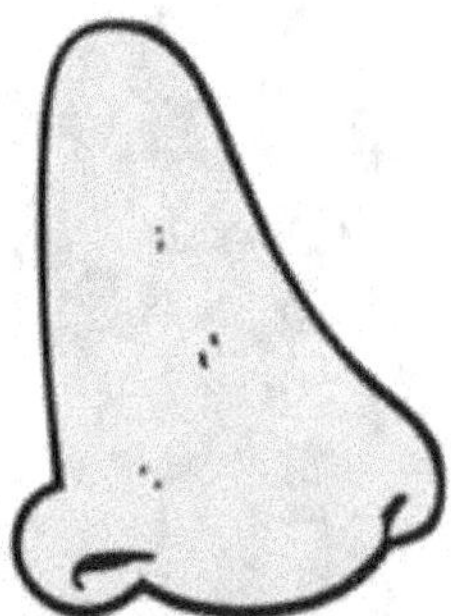

The nose smells something.

épaules

어깨

He puts his hands on his shoulders.

estomac

위

He has a big stomach.

les dents

이

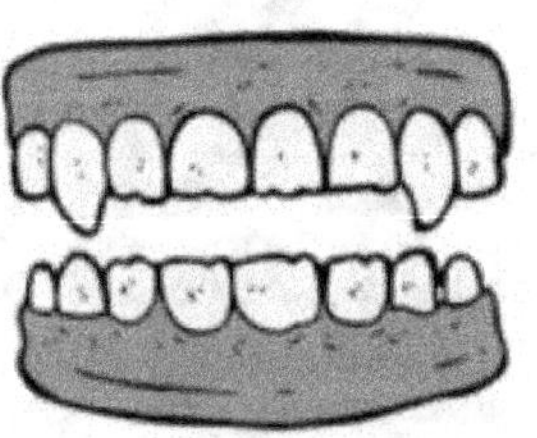

The teeth are clean and white.

gorge

목

He has a sore throat today.

les orteils

발가락

My toes are small.

langue

혀

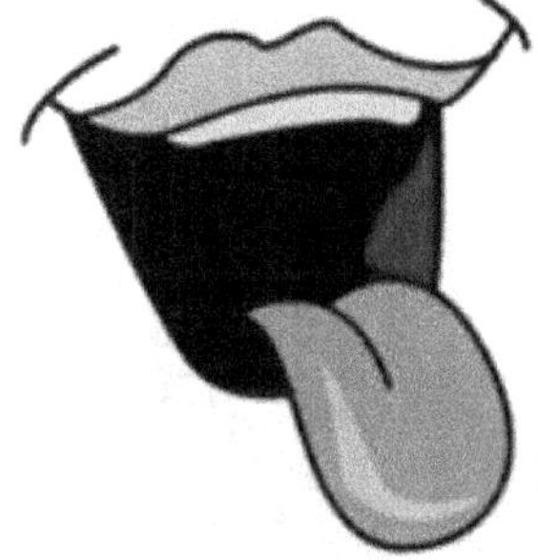

My tongue is licking ice cream.

dent

이

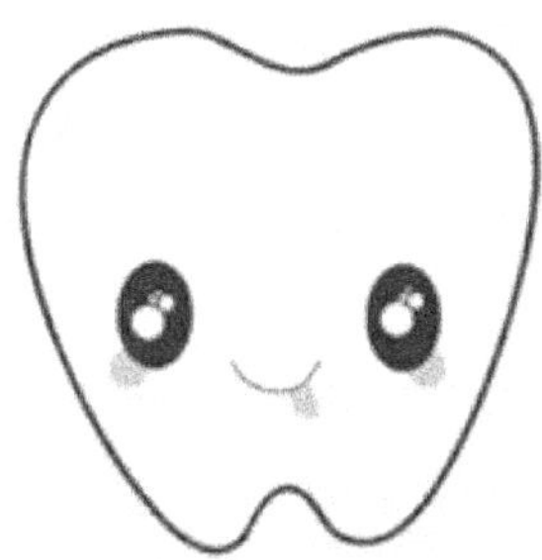

The tooth has big eyes.

taille

허리

He has his hands on his waist.

salopette

바지

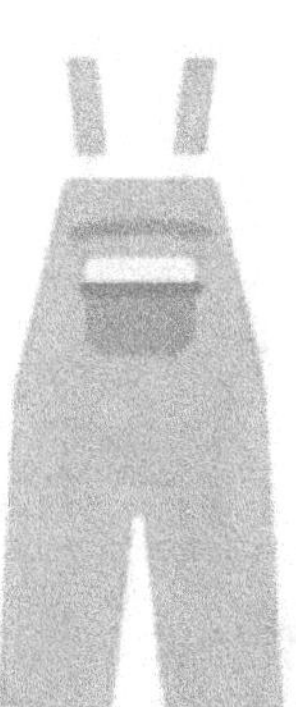

I bought these overalls for you!

mitaines

장갑

The mittens are very warm.

bonnet

비니

The beanie is for winter.

tablier

앞치마

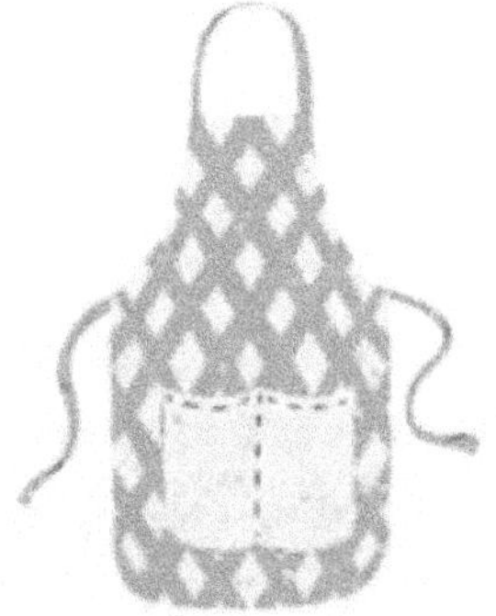

I wear my apron when I bake.

poupée

인형

The doll is for my baby sister.

hochets

딸랑이

The rattle is for the baby.

jouet

장난감

The toy is very fun.

couche

기저귀

The baby has to wear a diaper.

berceau

요람

She is sleeping in her bassinet.

bavoir

턱받이

My baby brother has to wear his
bib when he is eating.

octogone

팔각형

The octagon is saying okay!

triangle

삼각형

The triangle has three corners.

carré

광장

Square

The square has four sides.

cercle

원

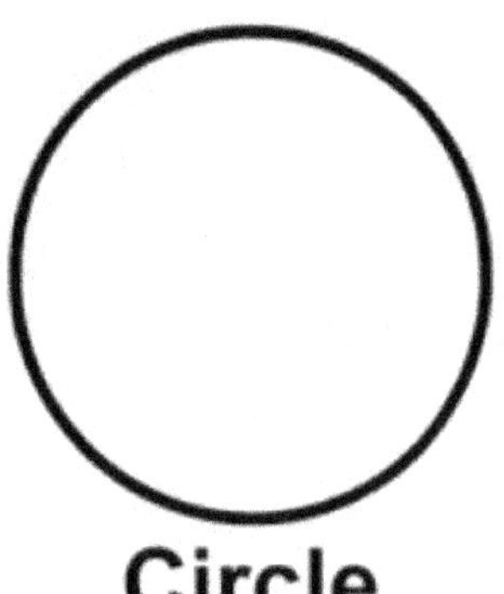

Circle

The circle is round.

ovale

타원

The oval shape looks like a circle.

cœur

심장

I drew a heart on my paper.

traverser

가로 질러 가다

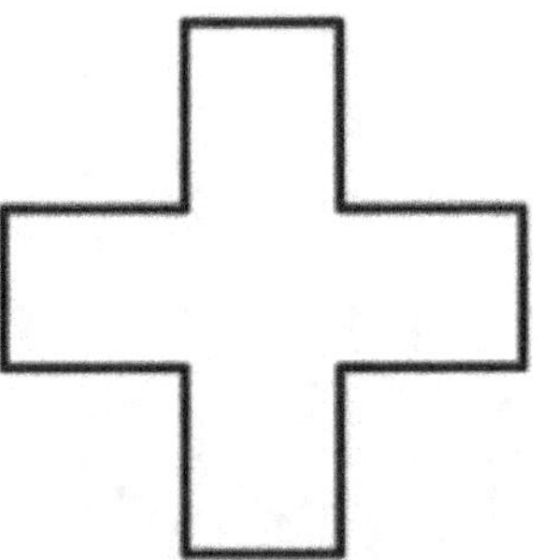

That sign is a cross.

la flèche

화살

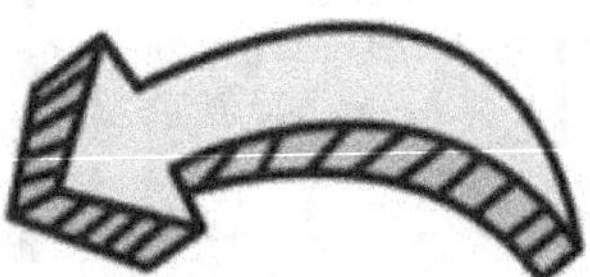

The arrow is pointing this way.

cube

입방체

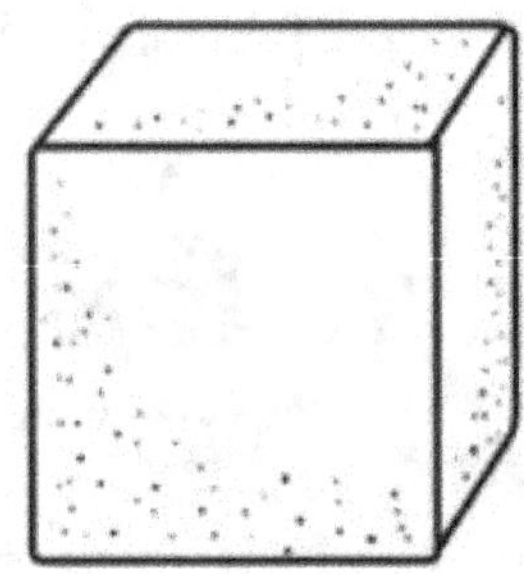

The cube is 3D.

étoile

별

The star is yellow and shiny.

tir à l'arc

양궁

The archery is where you aim.

badminton

배드민턴

My favorite sport is badminton.

criquet

크리켓

I am very good at cricket.

bowling

볼링

I got one pin down at bowling!

boxe

권투

The boxing gloves are hot.

tennis

테니스

He can hit the ball in tennis.

faire de la planche a roulettes

스케이트 보드

He skateboards to school.

planche de surf

서핑

The shark loves surfing in the ocean.

le hockey

하키

I like to play Ice hockey.

yoga

요가

He is closing his eyes and doing yoga.

épée

펜싱

They are fencing and dueling together.

aptitude

적합

She will do some fitness in the pool.

gymnastique

체조

He can do brilliant gymnastics.

karaté

카라테

She is good at kicking in Karate.

volley-ball

배구

She is holding a volleyball.

musculation

역도

The girl with brown hair can do weightlifting.

basketball

농구

He can balance the ball with one finger in basketball.

base-ball

야구

The little chick is in the finales at baseball.

le rugby

럭비

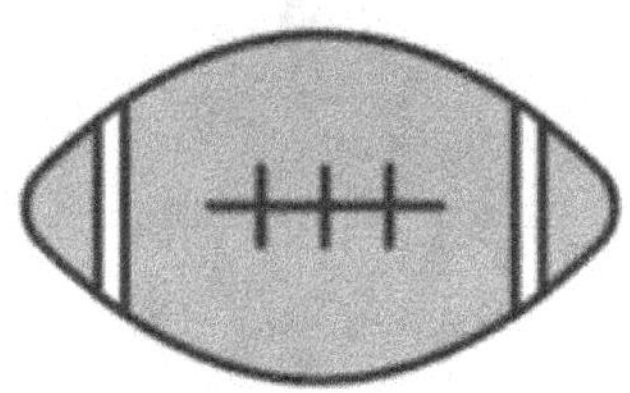

The rugby ball has white stripes.

lutte

레슬링

The sumo will compete in wrestling.

course de voitures

자동차 경주

He is number one for car racing.

cyclisme

사이클링

He is peacefully cycling on the road.

fonctionnement

달리는

He is running while listening to his earphones.

tennis de table

탁구

My brother and dad will play table tennis.

pêche

어업

He will go to the river to fish.

judo

유도

She has a red belt in Judo.

escalade

등산

He will climb the ladder.

tournage

촬영

He is shooting the archery board.

le golf

골프

She is going to compete in the golf competition.

balade

타기

He will ride his scooter.

asseyez-vous

앉아

They are sitting down together.

se lever

일어

She likes to stand up.

bats toi

싸움

They are fighting over the book.

rire

웃음

He is laughing so hard!

lis

읽다

She read a picture book.

jouer

플레이

He went to play on the slide.

ecoutez

들리다

He listened for the ice cream cart.

pleurer

울음 소리

He cried because he got a bad grade.

pense

생각한다

He thought that the test would be hard.

chanter

노래

He sang for the concert.

regarder la télévision

tv 시청

He watched TV the whole night.

danse

댄스

She was a good dancer.

allumer

켜다

The light is turned on.

éteindre

끄다

The light is turned off.

gagner

승리

He won the contest.

mouche

파리

The parrot can fly.

couper

절단

He was cutting his nails.

désinvolte

버리다

He threw away the garbage.

dormir

자다

He slept soundly.

fermer

닫기

He closed his mouth shut.

ouvert

열다

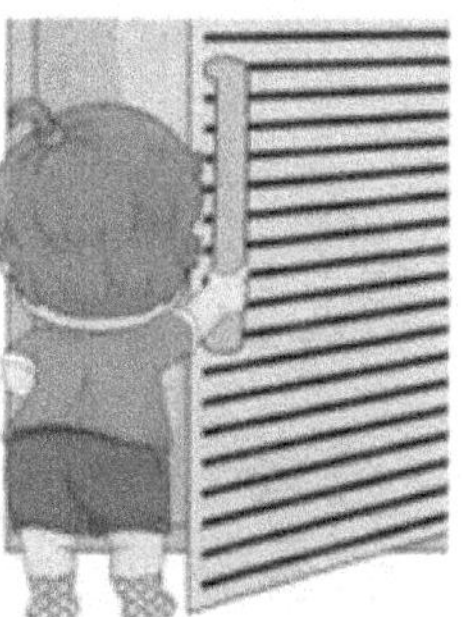

She opened the bathroom door.

écrire

쓰다

She wrote with a pencil.

donner

주기

Santa gave her a present.

sauter

도약

She had fun jumping.

manger

먹다

The shark ate yummy ice cream.

boisson

음주

The old British man drank tea.

cuisinier

쿡

The microwave cooked his soup.

lavage

빨래

You need to remember to wash
your hands.

attendre

기다림

He was waiting for the bus.

montée

상승

She climbed a lot of mountains.

parler

이야기

Two best friends were talking together.

crawl

포복

The baby crawled on the floor.

rêver

꿈

The Sloth dreamed about eating leaves.

creuser

파기

That strong man dug a swimming pool.

taper

박수

The baby clapped her hands.

tricoter

뜨다

She knits with the purple string.

coudre

꿰매다

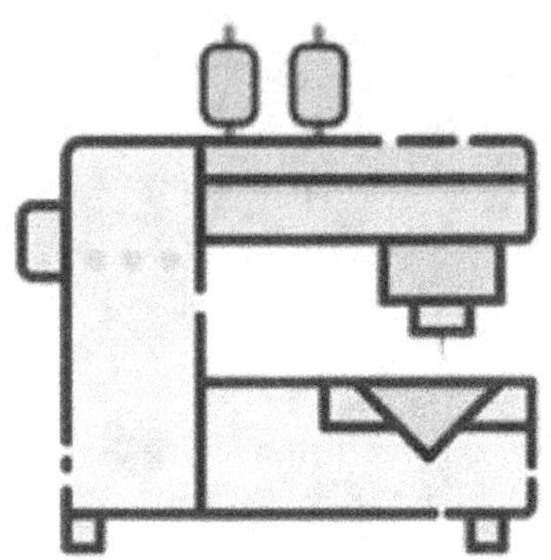

That is a sewing machine.

odeur

냄새

The perfume smelled great.

baiser

키스

He kissed his mother.

étreinte

포옹

They hugged each other.

ronfler

코골이

The tiger snored.

baigner

담그다

He took a bath.

s'incliner

운궁법

He bowed to the judge.

peindre

페인트

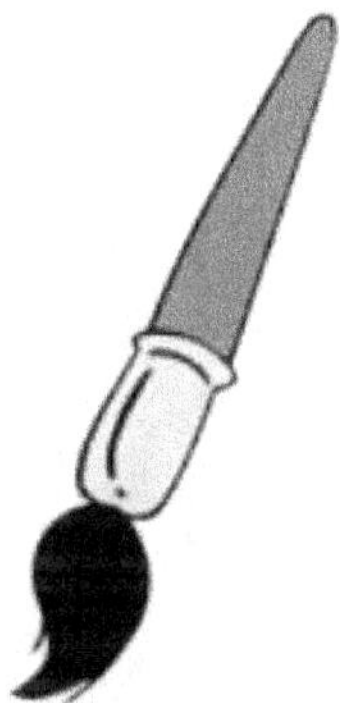

He painted a colorful picture.

se plonger

잠수

He dove to the deepest part of the ocean.

ski

스키

The ski was expensive.

empiler

스택

The books are stacked high.

acheter

구입

They bought cereal.

secouer

떨림

They shook hands together.

programmeur

프로그램 제작자

He was a smart computer programmer.

vétérinaire

수의사

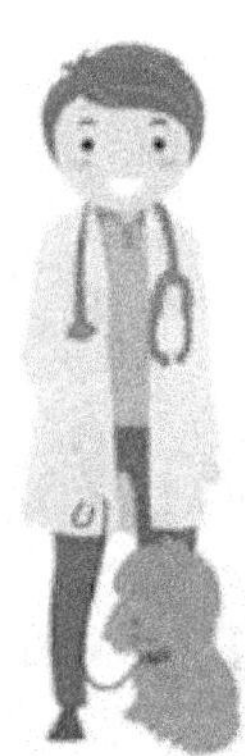

She is a veterinarian.

vendeur de rue

노점상

That street vendor sells hot dogs.

mineur

갱부

That Miner will find gold.

prof

선생님

The owl is the teacher.

groom

보이

That Bellboy is fat.

orateur

스피커

The chicken is a great Speaker.

boucher

푸줏간

The Butcher sells fish.

pharmacien

제약사

That Pharmacist saved a person's life.

réceptionniste

접수 원

He is a Receptionist.

politicien

정치가

He wants to be a Politician.

guide touristique

여행 가이드

That Tour guide led us around Japan.

entrepreneur

기업가

He is an Entrepreneur.

danseuse de ballet

발레 댄서

She is training to be a Ballet dancer.

astronaute

우주 비행사

He is a great astronaut.

juge

판사

That Judge is always fair.

avocat

변호사

The lawyer is serious.

la caissière

출납원

She is a cashier at the market.

conducteur de taxi

택시 운전사

He is a fast Taxi driver.

plombier

배관공

That Plumber fixes toilets.

musicien

음악가

She wants to be a Musician like her teacher.

chef

요리사

The chef makes fast food.

boulanger

빵 굽는 사람

That baker is a bread.

artiste

예술가

That Artist came from Italy.

acteur

배우

That actor is famous.

barman

바 키퍼

The Bartender works in a bar.

coiffeur

미용사

That girl is a Hairdresser.

évêques

주교

He is a Bishop.

opticien

안경점

She went to an Optician.

fleuriste

플로리스트

She is a great Florist.

écrivain

작가

He is a famous author.

comptable

회계사

My accountant is loyal.

du vin

포도주

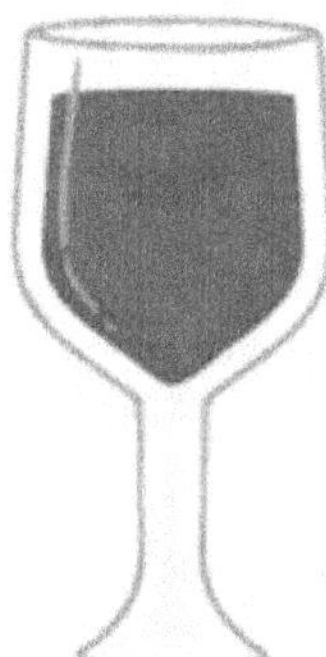

That wine tastes good.

café

커피

That coffee is bitter.

limonade

레몬 에이드

The lemonade is refreshing.

chocolat chaud

뜨거운 초콜릿

I drink hot chocolate every day.

milk-shake

밀크 쉐이크

The milkshake has whipped cream.

eau

물

The water is not cold.

thé

차

The tea is hot.

lait

우유

Milk is white.

bière

맥주

The beer is foamy.

un soda

탄산 음료

The soda is fizzy.

smoothie

점잖은 사람

The smoothie is a watermelon flavor.

milk-shake

밀크 쉐이크

The milkshake has whipped cream.

lait de coco

코코넛 우유

The coconut milk is yummy.

du jus d'orange

오렌지 주스

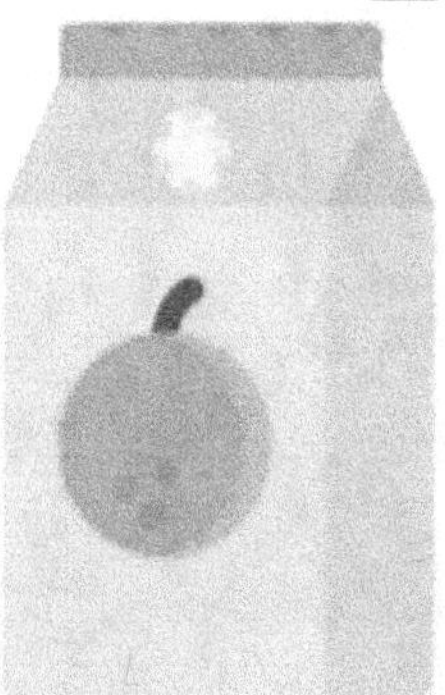

The orange juice is made from oranges.

cacao

코코아

The cocoa is sweet.

fromage

치즈

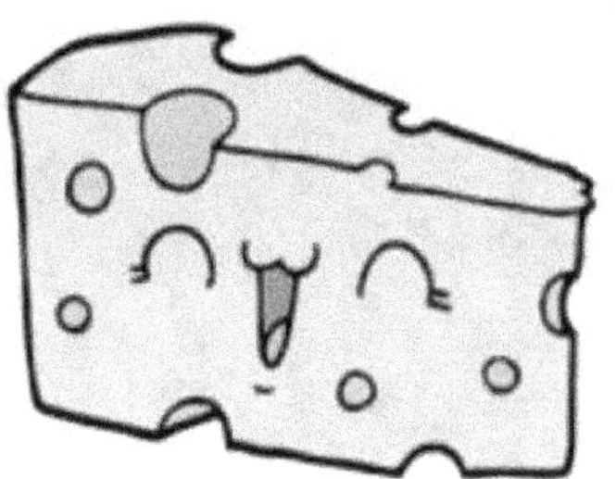

The cheese is creamy.

oeuf

계란

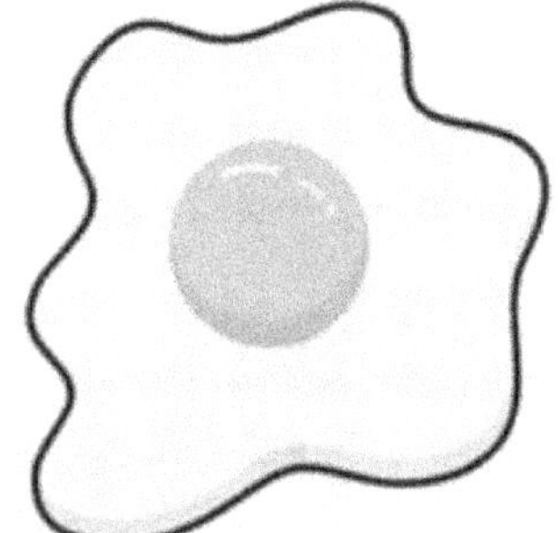

The egg is fried.

beurre

버터

The butter is put on bread.

margarine

마가린

Margarine looks like butter.

yaourt

요거트

That yogurt is popular.

cottage cheese

코티지 치즈

The cottage cheese is put on crackers.

crème glacée

아이스크림

They have a triple scoop ice cream.

crème

크림

That is a lot of creams.

sandwich

샌드위치

That sandwich is healthy.

saucisse

소시지

Americans love sausages.

hamburger

햄버거

That hamburger looks happy.

hot-dog

핫도그

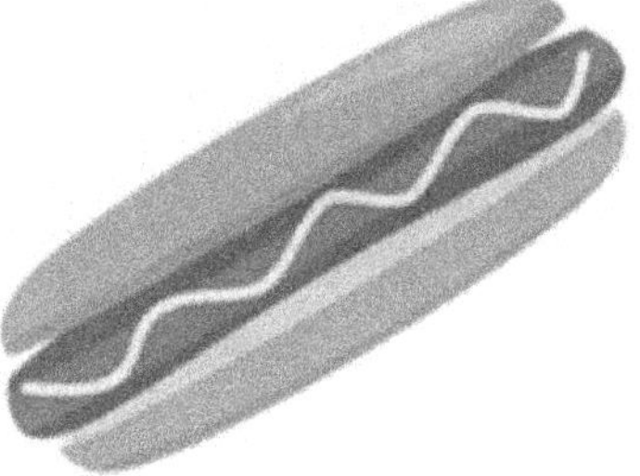

That hot dog has mustard on it.

pain

빵

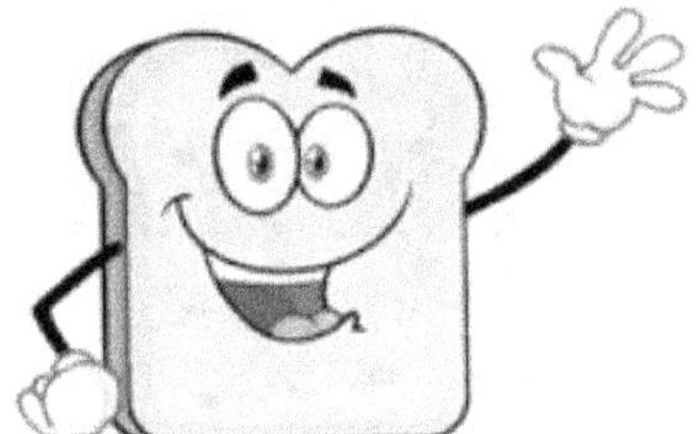

That bread is saying hello.

pizza

피자

That pizza is cheesy.

steak

스테이크

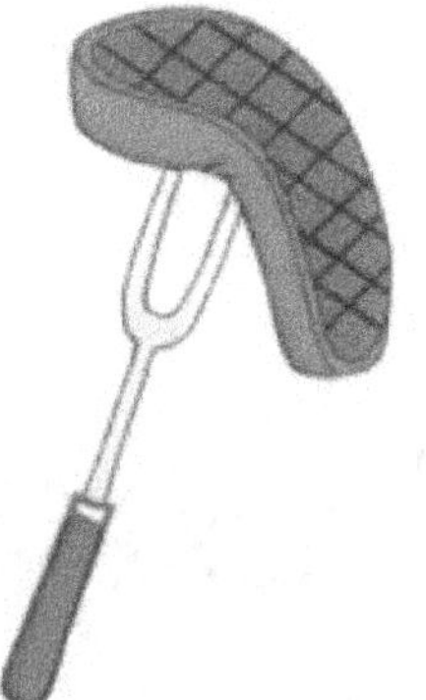

The steak was grilled.

poulet rôti

구운 치킨

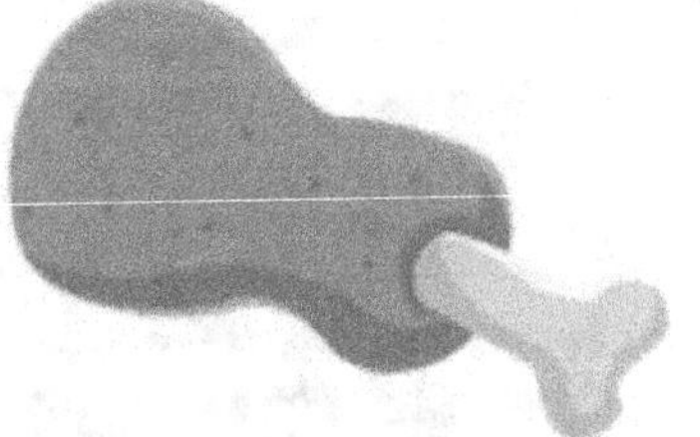

Roast Chicken is delicious.

poisson

물고기

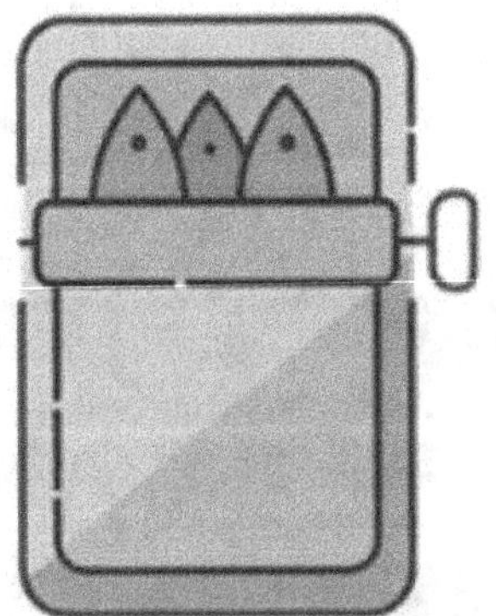

You can buy canned fish in the market.

fruit de mer

해물

Lobster is expensive seafood.

jambon

햄

Ham can be put in sandwiches.

kebab

케밥

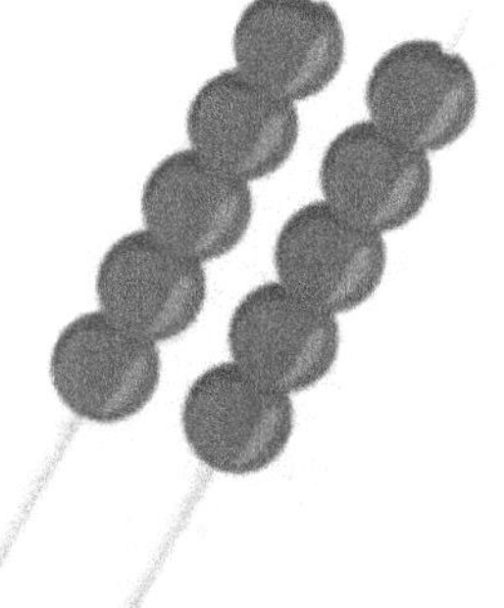

Kebab is a delicacy in America.

bacon

베이컨

That bacon is smiling.

crème fraîche

사워 크림

You can dip your chips in sour cream.

vache

소

Cows are black and white.

lapin

토끼

That rabbit is fun to play with.

canard

오리

That duck is content.

crevette

새우

The shrimp has six legs.

porc

돼지

That pig is pink and fat.

abeille

벌

The bee has a stinger.

chèvre

염소

That goat has a white horn.

crabe

게

The crab has two big pincers.

cerf

사슴

That deer is sleeping.

dinde

터키

The turkey has a giant tail.

colombe

비둘기

That dove is carrying a plant.

mouton

양

That sheep has fluffy wool.

poisson

물고기

That fish has colorful fins.

poulet

치킨

That chicken is waking everybody up.

cheval

말

The horse has a red mane.

chaise

의자

That wing chair is yellow.

meuble tv

tv 스탠드

The TV stand can hold books.

canapé

소파

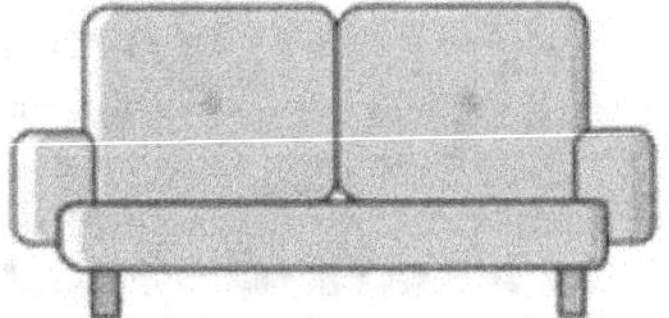

The sofa is comfortable to sit on.

coussins

쿠션

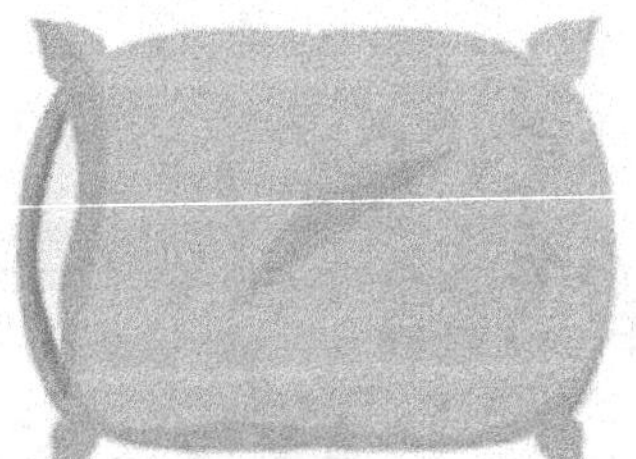

The cushion helps soften your seat.

téléphone

전화

The telephone is ringing.

télévision

텔레비전

That television is big.

haut-parleurs

연사

That speaker is used to increase the volume.

table d'appoint

사이드 테이블

That end table is sparkling clean.

service à thé

차 세트

That tea set is from China.

cheminée

난로

The fireplace makes me warm.

télécommandes

리모컨

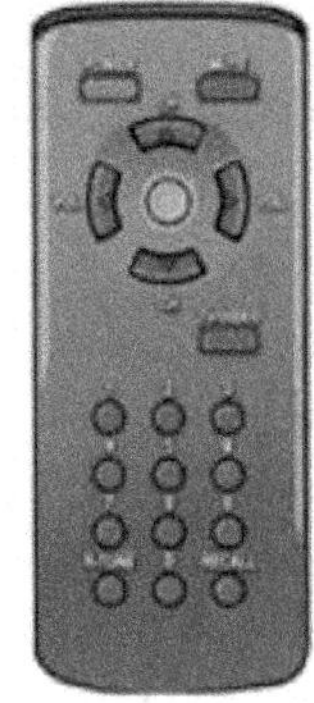

The remote has lots of buttons.

ventilateur électrique

선풍기

The fan is blowing wind.

lampadaire

플로어 램프

The floor lamp is very tall.

tapis

양탄자

The carpet is soft and silky.

bureaux

책상

The table is made of wood.

stores

블라인드

I will pull the blinds down.

rideaux

커튼

She opened the curtains.

image

그림

The picture is about the mountains and the sky.

vase

병 장식

The roses are all in a vase.

l'horloge

시계

The alarm clock is beeping.

oreiller

베개

The pillow is pink and yellow.

cintre

모자 걸이

The hat stand has only one hat on it.

mettre la table

화장대

I have made up on my dressing table.

lampe de table

테이블 램프

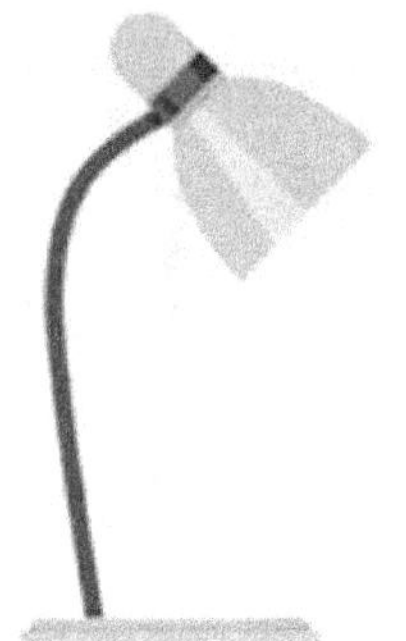

The table lamp will help me see in the dark.

miroir

거울

The mirror is very tall.

planche a repasser

다리미판

Don't touch the ironing board, it's hot!

boîte avec tiroir

서랍이있는 상자

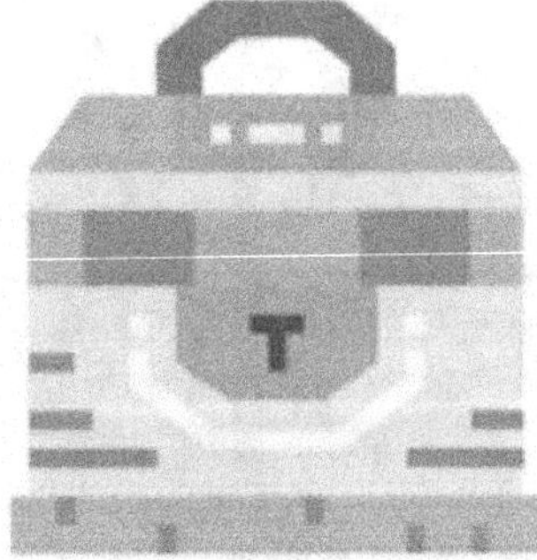

You can keep your clothes in the hope chest.

table de chevet

침대 탁자

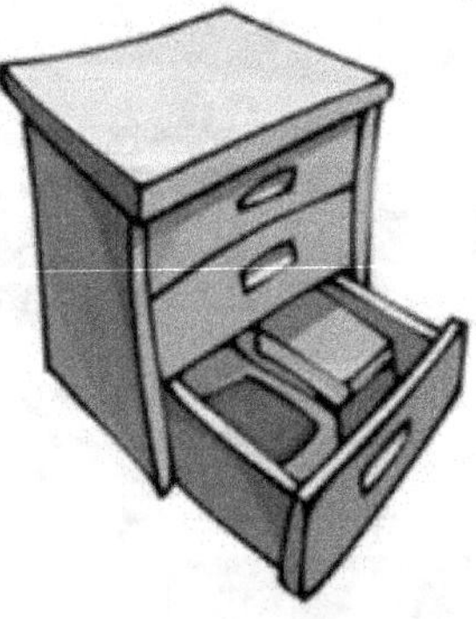

The nightstand has my lamp on it.

lit

침대

The bed is charming.

climatisation

에어컨

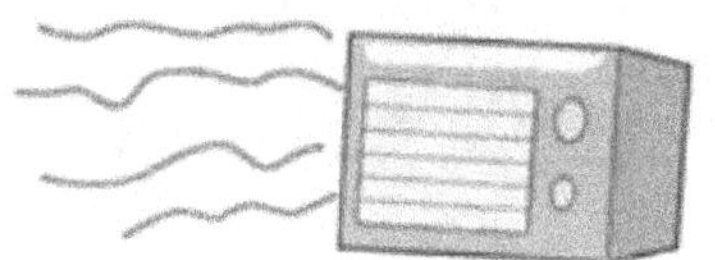

The air conditioner is cold.

cruche

조끼

The measuring jug has nothing inside.

dentifrice

치약

The toothpaste is mint flavored.

brosse à dents

칫솔

The toothbrush has toothpaste on it.

savon

비누

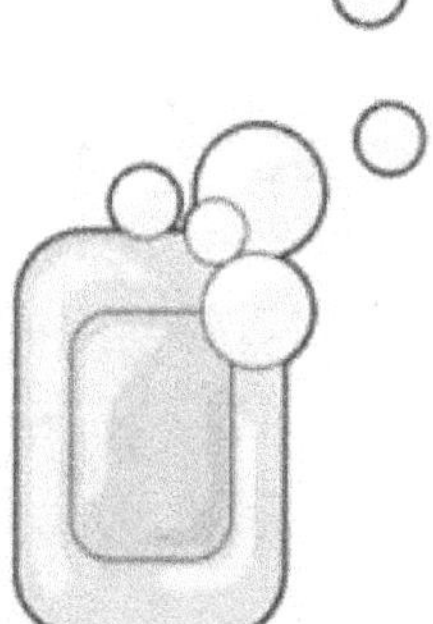

The soap is very bubbly.

pince à linge

빨래 집게

The clothespin will clip my clothes.

cintre

매다는 사람

The hanger is hanging my boots.

sèche-cheveux

헤어 드라이어

The hairdryer will blow my hair.

shampooing

샴푸

The shampoo is used to clean your hair.

bulle

거품

The bubbles are very fun to play in.

brosse

브러시

She is brushing her hair with the brush.

papier toilette

휴지

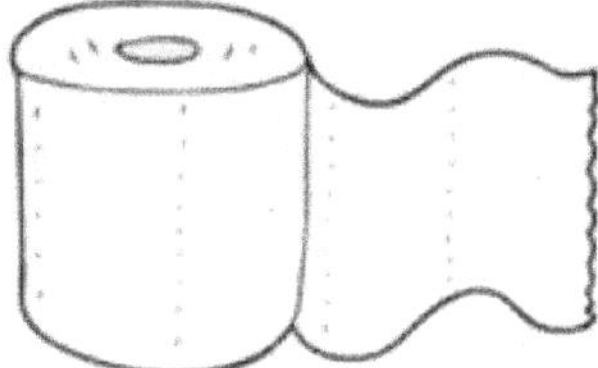

The toilet paper is used to dry your hands.

serviette

수건

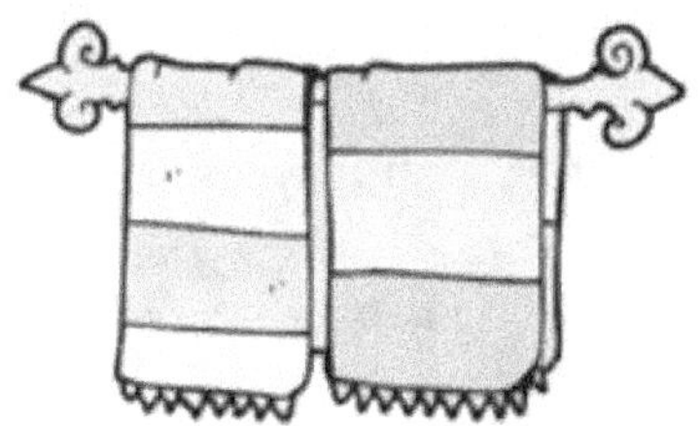

We have two towels on the rack.

corde à linge

빨랫줄

My shirt is hanging on the clothesline.

douche

샤워

The shower is spraying water.

baignoire

목욕통

The bathtub is comfortable.

lessive

세탁 세제

The laundry detergent is used with the washing machine.

seau

버킷

Can you help me fill up the bucket?

vadrouilles

걸레

The mop is used for mopping the floor.

savon liquide

액체 비누

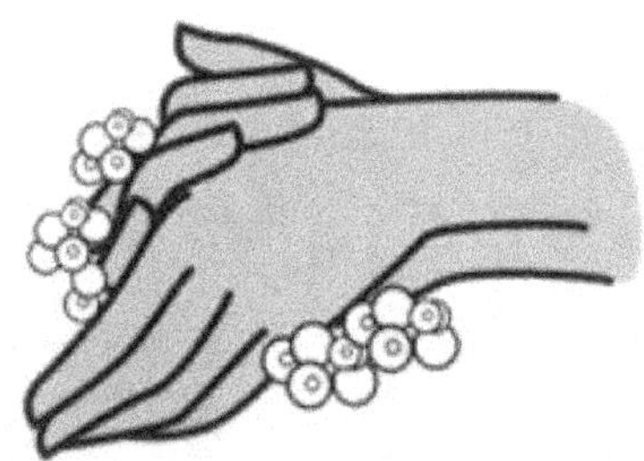

I use soapy water to wash my hands.

lessive en poudre

세탁 파우더

I will scoop up the washing powder.

sac poubelle

쓰레기 봉투

The trash bag is full of trash.

poubelle

쓰레기통

You have only to put recylcle trash in the trash can.

les puits

싱크

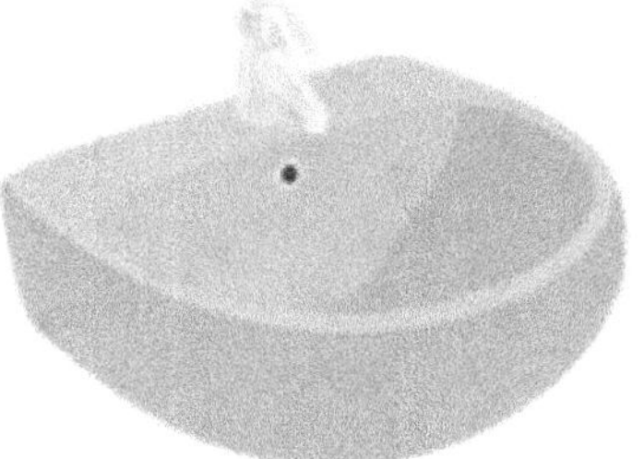

You should wash your hands in the sink.

cuvette des toilettes

변기

She let her bunny use the toilet.

machine à laver

세탁기

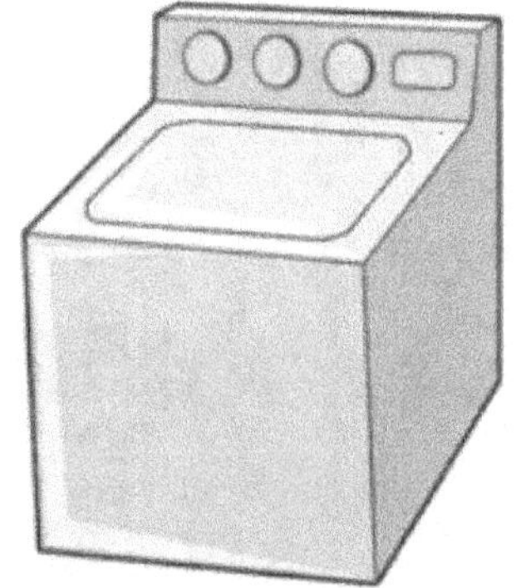

The washing machine wash your clothes.

panier à linge

세탁 바구니

She is putting all the clothes into the laundry basket.

le rasoir

면도칼

He uses the razor to shave his beard.

rasoir électrique

전기 면도기

The electric razor works faster than the normal one.

crème à raser

면 도용 크림

The shaving cream is fluffy.

bain de bouche

구강 청정제

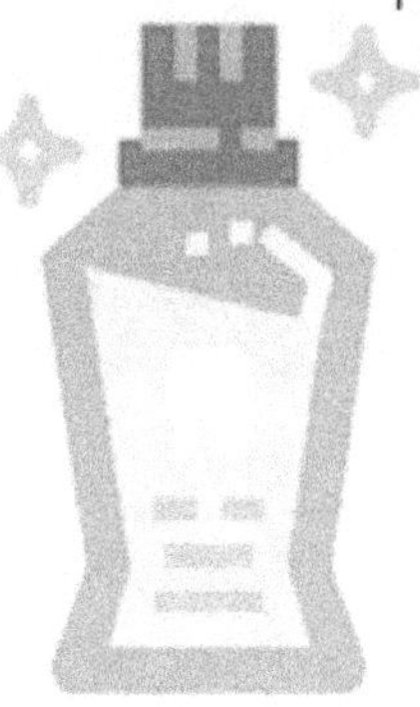

The mouthwash smells very lovely.

coton-tige

면봉

Q-tip can be used for many things.

brosse à cheveux

헤어 브러쉬

She brushes her hair with her hairbrush.

peigne

빗

Her dad will comb her hair for her.

nettoyant

세제

Put the cap back on the cleanser bottle.

échelle

규모

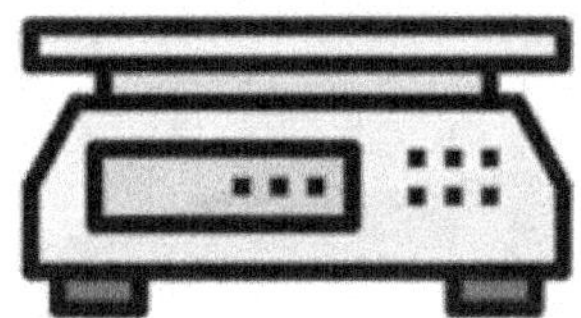

You can measure things on the scale.

papier de soie

티슈 페이퍼

The tissue is on the counter.

jouets de bain

목욕 완구

The little duck is a bath toy.

robinet

수도꼭지

The faucet is broken.

miroir

거울

He is looking in the mirror.

tapis de bain

욕실 깔개

The bath mat is purple and yellow.

www.ingramcontent.com/pod-product-compliance
Lightning Source LLC
Chambersburg PA
CBHW060516120726
48002CB00011B/3189